Complex Kids,
Simple Solutions

Complex Kids, Simple Solutions

How to raise resilient,
confident, likeable kids

Jenny Demark Ph.D.
Conrad Leung BCBA
& Linda Reinstein Ph.D.

First published 2025

Exisle Publishing Pty Ltd
C/o Shortland Chartered Accountants Ltd, Level 9, 51 Shortland Street, Auckland 1010, New Zealand
PO Box 864, Chatswood, NSW 2057, Australia
www.exislepublishing.com

Copyright © 2025 in text: Jenny Demark Ph.D., Conrad Leung BCBA & Linda Reinstein Ph.D.

Jenny Demark Ph.D., Conrad Leung BCBA & Linda Reinstein Ph.D. assert the moral right to be identified as the authors of this work.

All rights reserved. Except for short extracts for the purpose of review, no part of this book may be reproduced, stored in a retrieval system or transmitted in any form or by any means, whether electronic, mechanical, photocopying, recording or otherwise, without prior written permission from the publisher.

A CiP record for this book is available from the National Library of Australia.

ISBN 978-1-923011-25-0

Designed by Bee Creative
Typeset in PT Serif, 10.5pt
Printed by Lightning Source

This book uses paper sourced under ISO 14001 guidelines from well-managed forests and other controlled sources.

10 9 8 7 6 5 4 3 2 1

Disclaimer

This book is a general guide only and should never be a substitute for the skill, knowledge and experience of a qualified medical professional's assessment of the facts, circumstances and symptoms of a particular child. The information presented in this book is based on the training and professional experiences of the authors, and is true and complete to the best of their knowledge. However, this book is intended only as an informative guide; it is not intended to replace or countermand the advice given by the qualified professionals supporting the readers. The authors, publishers and their distributors are not responsible for any adverse effects or consequences resulting from the use of information in this book. It is the responsibility of the reader to consult qualified professionals regarding the personal care of their children. The intent of the information provided is to be helpful; however, there is no guarantee of results associated with the information provided.

Dr Jenny Demark is a Child Clinical Psychologist whose goal is to improve the quality of life for children and their families by sharing the insights of **Prepare. Teach. Motivate**. She has decades of experience working with children, youth, parents and schools, and she is known for her warm and collaborative approach to skill building. Dr Demark enjoys outdoor activities, eating gourmet food and maintaining a net-zero energy home with her husband, two sons and rescue dog.

Conrad Leung is a Board Certified Behaviour Analyst who is passionate about helping people. He has worked with diverse families and a variety of professionals in homes, schools, clinical and group care settings. He strives to translate principles and research into solutions that produce meaningful changes in the lives of children, their families and those who support them. He also supports and supervises future Behaviour Analysts. In his spare time, Conrad enjoys learning from his young children, cooking from scratch and listening to good music.

Dr Linda Reinstein is a Child Clinical and School Psychologist with a broad range of experience in understanding, assessing and consulting about complex developmental, learning and behavioural issues. She strives to help parents and children make meaningful changes in their relationships and lives through collaboration, connection, skill development and compassion. When not working in her private practice, she enjoys spending time with her husband and two teenage children.

Contents

Introduction 1

Section I — Prepare 5
1. Setting the Stage 6
2. Quality Time: A powerful PREPARE strategy 31

Section II — Teach 45
3. Being a 'Skills Detective'...46
4. TEACHing..62

Section III — Motivate 83
5. Understanding Reinforcement...84
6. Understanding Punishment 118

Section IV — Prepare. Teach. Motivate. in Action 153
7. Just Do It! Teaching co-operation................................. 154
8. You Can't Always Get What You Want: Teaching your child to cope when you say no or ask them to wait 183

9. Getting Out the Door: Taking the 'mad' out of the mad dash in the morning 199

10. Giving It Up: Teaching your child to transition away from screens 206

11. We Can Handle This Together: Helping your child manage their big emotions 224

12. To Sleep, Perchance to … Actually Sleep! Teaching your child to sleep in their own bed for the whole night 244

Concluding Remarks 271

Acknowledgements 273

References 275

Index 280

Introduction

Simple does not mean easy.

Parenting is by far one of the most challenging and probably one of the most rewarding jobs that we are never, ever prepared for! Our babies do not come with manuals. Everyone has advice.

In today's world, with its myriad information and misinformation available at the click of a button, it has never been more confusing to know how to raise children to be resilient, confident and likeable. Many people giving parenting advice today do not have backgrounds in child development, clinical psychology, nor in the science of learning and behaviour change. Nonetheless, they have built almost cult-like followings on social media and are doggedly devoted to ideas that may or may not be helpful for healthy child development.

So, what is a parent to do?

Complex Kids, Simple Solutions: How to raise resilient, confident, likeable kids is grounded in science and guided by what the research tells us would be good practice. It is not easy. But it is simple. And it's based on three fundamental ideas: **Prepare. Teach. Motivate.**

Whether the child has a diagnosis of ADHD, Autism Spectrum Disorder, Oppositional Defiant Disorder or is just giving their parents a good run for their money, we are offering a unique and straightforward parenting perspective. Weaving together theories from the fields of developmental, cognitive and clinical psychology, with the practical, 'roll-up your sleeves and get it done' approach of Applied Behaviour Analysis (the science of behaviour), no other book has blended the expertise from these disciplines into one coherent parenting framework.

Complex Kids, Simple Solutions explains how three fundamental concepts apply to almost any situation parents may encounter, from the mundane to the meltdown. Once these fundamental concepts are understood and mastered, parents will be able to tackle with confidence, precision and consistency almost anything their child may throw at them. And yes, their child may actually *throw* things at them! We know from our collective clinical and lived experiences that the consistent implementation of these fundamentals will lead to resilient, confident and likeable kids.

The first parenting fundamental is to **Prepare**. Prepare yourself and prepare your child. Plan ahead and be strategic. Pick the right battles upfront. Set the stage for parenting success. Parents will learn how to validate their children's perspectives, opinions and feelings without necessarily agreeing or 'giving in' before teaching and motivating them to behave in resilient, confident and likeable ways. One of the single best proactive strategies available to parents is to spend *Quality Time* building and maintaining a strong connection with their child, a topic so important that we devote an entire

INTRODUCTION

chapter to it. Our approach is warm, collaborative and kind, and it requires parents and kids to be well-connected.

The second fundamental is to directly **Teach** children the skills they are lacking. Shifting away from a 'bad behaviour' paradigm, our approach refocuses parents to understand misbehaviour in terms of missing skills. Many parenting challenges arise because a child does not have a specific skill, be it co-operation, accepting being told no or waiting their turn. Here the parenting task is two-fold. First, parents must be able to clearly identify and define the missing skill. Second, parents have to teach that skill. Our book guides parents through every step of this process.

Finally, the third fundamental is to **Motivate**. Our approach teaches parents how to motivate their children to be resilient, confident and likeable. Motivation can be used to improve skills such as using manners, sleeping through the night and co-operating with requests. It can also be used to decrease unwanted behaviours such as tantrums, whining and defiance. *Complex Kids, Simple Solutions* gives parents the confidence in their reactions, without waffling, 'giving-in' or second-guessing their every move. We show parents how to plan for their use of consequences, whether they be rewards or punishments. Spoiler alert: *Complex Kids, Simple Solutions* promotes the use of rewards over punishments to motivate children.

We have reviewed the research and we have applied it successfully in our work with thousands of families. *Complex Kids, Simple Solutions* is presented as a reader-friendly guide to raising resilient, confident and likeable kids. Key information is provided in easy-to-follow points, with a good dose of humour and humility. We've included meaningful examples to illustrate how **Prepare. Teach. Motivate.**

strategies can be used. Several chapters provide parents and clinicians with guides and considerations for putting the material into practice. We strongly recommend you create a Parenting Journal for yourself to take notes, make plans and individualize the ideas from the practical 'Putting it into Practice' sections. And for those wanting to know more about the 'geeky' science behind *Complex Kids, Simple Solutions*, plenty of sidebars are provided throughout.

Time to roll up your sleeves.

Enjoy!

SECTION I

—

Prepare

1.
Setting the Stage

We have all heard that it is better to be proactive than reactive. We know that investing time upfront saves us hassles later on. A stitch in time saves nine … etcetera, etcetera, etcetera. But, as parents, we have very busy lives. We make cupcakes for the bake sale. We volunteer for school field trips. We carpool to soccer practices, hockey rinks and swim meets. We throw birthday parties. We drive to the mall and to the movies. We show up on time for language lessons, tutoring and a whole host of other activities. We do all these things not because we love every minute of them but because we want to ensure our kids have rich, healthy and fulfilling lives.

Put on top of that the daily responsibilities of cooking, cleaning, preparing lunches and going to your paid work. Now sprinkle in the complexities and realities of our actual children — our children who do not always behave the way we want and need them to, when we want them to or need them to.

1. SETTING THE STAGE

This sometimes means there is not a lot of time to get ahead of things. We get it. We live it. Parenting is tough!

Parents simply do not have the time to be as prepared as they would like to be. We fall prey to marketing strategies aimed to guilt us into feeling disorganized, unprepared and wasteful of our precious family time. We do not need more suggestions on meal prep and sticky-note organizers to make ourselves more available to our families.

Let's be clear. This is NOT our message.

Our message is simple. Taking a few moments ahead of time to **Prepare** for interactions with our kids will actually save time and frustration in the end. And much of this preparation is mental preparation — not time taken to buy, make or create things.

> **CAN YOU RELATE?**
>
> Penelope argues with her mother about taking a bath. Her mum hears 'I don't want to' for the umpteenth time and is already feeling tired from her hectic day at the office.
>
> **RESULT:** Her mum decides to skip the bath altogether and is frustrated that she relented to her daughter's strong will yet again.
>
> Joseph's father offers to help with homework. At first, things are going very well but when they move onto a new topic, Joseph immediately complains that it is 'too hard'. Joseph hides under the table and refuses to keep working.

RESULT: Fed up, his father walks away from the table and the homework does not get finished. His dad is worried Joseph will fail his upcoming test.

Claude and his brother Philippe balk at the broccoli on their dinner plates. One of them goes so far as to throw his greens on the floor.

RESULT: His mother picks up the broccoli from the floor, 'gives in' and allows them to not eat their vegetables. She spends the rest of the evening upset with herself, feeling guilty and like a 'bad parent' for not being able to feed her children healthy foods.

Anjali is told she can watch one episode of her favourite show after dinner. After the show ends, she sits quietly, hoping her parents will not notice it is over. When her parents enter the room 10 minutes later, Anjali is happily engaged in the second episode.

RESULT: Parents are upset about her lack of honesty but they decide to 'let it go' and let her keep watching as she is already halfway through the episode. They feel guilty and discouraged about the amount of screen time they are allowing.

Remember these kiddos and their parents. We will re-visit them at the end of the chapter.

Maybe not all of these scenarios are familiar, but they all have a common thread. In each one, the parents are *reactive* in response to their children's complaints, resistance or refusals. Each scenario illustrates parents' attempts to avoid, limit or shorten conflicts. And, in each scenario, parents are left feeling guilty, worried and frustrated.

Don't misunderstand. There is nothing wrong with trying to reduce the arguing and fighting in the household. That is our goal too. However, we suggest there are other ways to go about it. All the above situations could have ended on a more positive note. Had parents used **Prepare** strategies to 'set the stage' for success, all parties would feel more satisfied, competent and connected.

Being Proactive: It's a MINDSET

Being proactive while parenting is fundamental. But we also know the word 'proactive' can strike fear and panic into many parents who feel they do not have the time to be more organized. So, before we get into what being proactive is and could look like, let's talk about what we do *not* mean.

We are *not* talking about simplified notions of the right meal prep strategy or colour-coded scheduling systems as the cure-all for making parenting easier.

Being prepared is *not* about being able to predict and be ready for every situation like a model Boy Scout. We are also not advocating a parenting approach whose aim is to never let our children experience hardships, disappointments or anger toward us.

Being proactive does *not* mean being protective, helicoptering or lawnmowering, or walking on eggshells to avoid a tantrum.

We are talking about a parenting mindshift, a parenting mindset.

» Being proactive means preparing our children to accept and follow our suggestions, directions and corrections.
» Being proactive means buying yourself time, if only for a moment, before making your parenting decisions about how to deal with any given situation.
» Being proactive means putting some money in the bank of goodwill with compliments, attention and noticing the 'good stuff'.
» Being proactive means being predictable for our kids when life does not stop throwing curveballs.

We are talking about preparing our kids to be the resilient, confident and likeable beings we want them to be.

Prepare

Let's discuss some specific ways to **Prepare** your child for success. Based on our experience and the research on child development and learning, we have found the following strategies to be highly effective in supporting kids to do the next right thing:

Pare it Down: Be realistic and pick your battles.

Be Clear: Spell it out, offer choices and provide a 'heads-up'.

1. SETTING THE STAGE

Give like a Grandparent: Be nice about it, provide freebies and catch them being good.

Pare it Down: Be Realistic and Pick Your Battles

Be realistic

Although it may not seem like it, all children will demonstrate challenging behaviours from time to time. Even your child's seemingly always well-behaved classmates, Perfect Pete and his sister Superb Sally, will have challenging behaviours at some point. Remember, **you know your child the best**. Accept them for where and who they are and keep guiding them forward. Avoid making comparisons to other children, *particularly those who you think are more perfect than your own*. Reflect on the progress your child has made. Compare them to their previous selves.

Preparing means being realistic about what your child can do, in any given situation, at any particular time.

> **CAN YOU RELATE?**
>
> Juanita's dad has spent an hour preparing a perfect family dinner. He has been looking forward to having the family sit together, eat, catch up and enjoy some conversation. Within fifteen minutes of calling everyone to the table, Juanita and her younger brother have finished their meals and are asking to be excused. Dad has barely started his own meal.

> **RESULT:** Juanita's dad feels frustrated that the family has already disbanded and he has not had the family meal he had envisioned or wanted.

Being realistic may require you to re-think your expectations. In the above example, it may be that the dad needs to re-think what it means to sit for a 'full meal'. While he may have wished his children would sit at the table for an hour, they might not be able to do so ... *yet*.

It is not reasonable to expect a young child, or a particularly energetic older child, to sit at the dinner table with family for an entire hour. However, it may be realistic for that child to sit at the table for fifteen minutes until they have eaten their food and told you about their day. Problem solved! You and your child are now feeling successful at dinner rather than frustrated, all because of a small shift in your expectations.

If you want everyone to wait until you start your meal, or if you want your children to be able to sit at the dinner table for a longer time, you will need to **Teach** them these specific skills. For strategies on how to do this, be patient and wait to read about **Teach** in the coming chapters.

1. SETTING THE STAGE

Pick your battles

CAN YOU RELATE?

Yusef usually cleans up his toys at the end of the day. However, today is a bit different. Today he had a playdate with his best friend. After a fun time playing and lots of sugary treats, Yusef is still wound up long after his friend has left. His room is littered with all his toys so his mother asks him to tidy up. Yusef refuses and has an epic meltdown.

RESULT: Yusef's mother cleans up the toys and threatens that he will never be able to have another playdate.

In the example above, Yusef's mother was reactive. She reacted to his refusal and tantrum. Her frustration led to threats she likely will not keep. Had she taken a moment to pick her battles, she may have realized this would not be a great day to ask Yusef to tidy his things by himself. Knowing this, she may have started cleaning up his toys for him and chatting with him about the fun he had with his friend while passing him toys to put away on the shelf.

Picking your battles means being mindful of the expectations, requests and instructions you give to your child. Think of when and where you give them, how often you give them and even what tone of voice you are using. Also keep in mind other factors such as fatigue, illness and hunger that can tip the balance of whether your child is likely to co-operate.

So, even when you know your child can do a particular task or chore, such as cleaning up the toys, there may be extenuating circumstances that make it harder for them to get the job done. Like Yusef in the above example, your child may be too 'wired or tired' to be able to co-operate at the end of a long day. You, the parent, may not have the energy or wherewithal to deal with an argument, stay calm and follow through with your request. It is perfectly okay to *not* ask Yusef to clean up after his fun-filled and exhausting day. You could simply clean it up for him or, better yet, leave the mess for tomorrow.

While we do not advocate tip-toeing around your children to avoid upsetting them, nor do we advocate removing all expectations, we do advise that you be realistic. Be realistic about how likely it is your child will listen, given unusual circumstances. Set them up for success. Pick your battles carefully. It is perfectly okay to *not* ask your child to do something you know they *can* do, but are *unlikely* to do because of extenuating circumstances.

Let's walk through a few scenarios to see what *picking your battles* might look like in different situations.

CAN YOU RELATE?

John's mum is working from home. She has an important phone conference she must attend in fifteen minutes. She notices that John, her twelve-year-old son, is on his phone and not doing the homework in a subject he needs help with.

1. SETTING THE STAGE

So now John's mother has to decide how to handle this situation. Knowing she cannot be late for her phone conference, she has a few options:

» Does she shout downstairs for John to get off his phone and start his homework?
» Does she ignore that she noticed him on his phone when he is supposed to be 'at school'?
» Could she implement a **Prepare** strategy or two ahead of time?

If she calls him to start his homework but she is not there to help him, it will not go well. He may begin a long diatribe about how unfair his teacher is. He may spiral into his worries about failing the course. He may tell his mother that he will start right away when in fact he probably will not because he cannot. If she pretends not to see him on his phone, she may be encouraging him to 'sneak' time on social media or technology when he is not supposed to be using it.

The prepared parent may have more success by letting John know she has a phone conference in fifteen minutes and she will be available in one hour to help him start his work. This way she acknowledges she knows what he is doing, she gives time-limited permission to stay on his phone until she is available, and she makes a plan with him to get his work done.

> **CAN YOU RELATE?**
>
> The Smiths have a very strict 'no screens' rule on weekdays. Their four-year-old son, Thelonious, is home from school with the flu. Thelonious is very bored and he has run out of ideas to keep himself busy. His dad, who has volunteered to work from home today, also has a tight deadline to meet.

So what is Mr Smith to do?

- » He could stand his ground and enforce the 'no screens' rule.
- » He could abandon work altogether to entertain Thelonious.
- » Could he implement a **Prepare** strategy or two?

If Dad enforces the 'no screens' rule, this will lead to a day full of battling with Thelonious to find things to do while attempting to get his work done. If he abandons his work altogether to entertain Thelonious, he will miss his deadline.

The prepared parent could allow Thelonious to watch a few of his favourite episodes in the afternoon while Dad finishes a report that is due by the end of the day.

Parents should have rules for their children, and these rules should be enforced. Yet there are times when the rules are meant to be broken. Parents (not the kids) can choose to **Prepare** for a successful day by letting go of certain rules in extenuating circumstances. Having a sick child at home is an appropriate time to let a battle go.

1. SETTING THE STAGE

> **CAN YOU RELATE?**
>
> Zena's after dinner 'job' is to walk the dog for fifteen minutes. This evening, dinner was later than anticipated. Zena has a quickly approaching swim team practice.

Her parents have a choice here:

- » They could force her to follow through with her job.
- » They could argue with her about completing her chores and then 'let her off the hook' to get to the swim team practice on time.
- » Are there **Prepare** strategies they could implement?

If they force her to follow through with her job, she will be late for her swim team and her coach may lecture her for letting down the team. If her parents let her off the hook after an argument, Zena may learn that she gets what she wants when she argues.

The prepared parent sees a third choice. They could choose to forgo this battle. Before asking Zena to do her chores, Dad could offer to do them for her, while Mum drives Zena to swim team practice. Offering to walk the dog as a favour sets Zena up for success. There is no arguing over chores. Zena is thankful to her parents and ready to resume her responsibilities the next day.

Be realistic. Pick your battles.

Be Clear: Spell it Out, Offer Choices and Provide a Heads-Up

Spell it out

We have just just explained why setting reasonable and achievable expectations for your child is important.

Now we want to emphasize that effective expectations are clear and concrete. Being clear and concrete means envisioning what your child would be doing if they were doing it right. If you were a fly on the wall, what would you see? Define and be clear about it. You may catch yourself having vague expectations such as 'I want my daughter to be respectful' or 'My son has to be kind'. While these are reasonable ideals, what would it actually look like if your daughter was 'being respectful' and your son was 'being kind'?

> **SCIENCE SIDEBAR**
>
> In geeky behavioural-speak, 'spelling it out' is called an Operational Definition. It precisely describes what we do and do not want to see. Operational Definitions avoid abstract terms and stick to observable behaviours.

For example, a child may not fully understand what is meant by 'respect'. The interpretation of respect may even be different between adults or between situations. This will require clarity of your expectations of 'respect' such as: taking off shoes when coming inside, speaking in sentences, not swearing, or doing what is asked by Mum and Dad. If your child does some of these things, recognize and celebrate the ways they are consistently respectful and **Teach** them the skills they need to be respectful in other situations.

> **CAN YOU RELATE?**
>
> Sanfred's parents place high value on table manners. They find themselves constantly nagging their children to 'use their manners'. This inevitably leads to an unpleasant family mealtime that is the opposite of what his parents intended.

Proper table manners vary between households and cultures. Rather than saying Sanfred should 'use his manners', his parents need to *spell it out* by giving a clear description of what they would like to see. This might be chewing with his mouth closed, using his napkin rather than his trousers to wipe his hands, and using utensils to eat rather than using his fingers.

Offer choices

Think about your child's typical day. They *have to* go to school. To do this, they *have to* get up on time, they *have to* eat breakfast, they *have to* catch the bus. At school, they *have to* sit in their seat, they *have to* raise their hand, they *have to* do their work. At home, they *have to* eat meals, they *have to* brush their teeth, they *have to* do their homework. From their perspective, their list of 'have tos' may feel endless.

Everyone appreciates having some control over their lives. Parents do. Children do. As the list above suggests, there are very few opportunities for children to have a say during their typical day.

Give *choices* when you can. Do it often. Do it consistently.

This will **Prepare** your child to be more co-operative. It sets the stage for making the 'have tos' more tolerable, more enjoyable and more manageable.

While it is not an option to skip breakfast, it is possible to offer choices such as which cereal they would like, or if they would like eggs or waffles. While taking a bath is not an option, you may be able to offer which bathroom they want to use, what type of shampoo they use and which bath toys they can bring. You can also have them choose if they want to do their homework before or after the bath. And where would they like to do their homework? You get the idea.

When giving choices, be sure each choice is actually available and acceptable in that particular situation at that particular time.

CAN YOU RELATE?

How likely are you to spend time with a friend who lets you *choose* the restaurant or the movie?

How likely are you to spend time with a friend who *never* lets you choose the restaurant or the movie?

1. SETTING THE STAGE

How likely are you to spend time with a friend who lets you choose the restaurant but then *finds a reason why they don't want to go* to the several restaurants that you suggest?

Having choices matters.

Provide a heads-up

The *Cambridge Dictionary* defines the term 'heads-up' as giving advance warning of something to come, usually so that we can prepare for it. In baseball, this term alerts outfielders to prepare for incoming balls. As adults, we appreciate getting a heads-up to prepare for unexpected or unplanned events.

> **CAN YOU RELATE?**
>
> You have worked for the last hour getting dinner ready for your family. Your partner calls to say they are going to be late. Then they arrive with an unexpected dinner guest — the boss.
>
> **RESULT:** Your kids are starving and you are furious!

A simple heads-up from your partner could have averted the stressful dinner and the argument that ensued after the boss's departure.

For kids, a heads-up is a powerful tool in the prepared parent's toolkit. A heads-up can prepare children to transition from one activity to another, to accept changes in daily routines, to adjust to unexpected fun events and to deal with the disappointment of plans getting cancelled. The heads-up helps to mentally prepare for what is to come. Sometimes saying, 'We're leaving the park in five minutes', 'Swimming is cancelled for tomorrow', 'This is the last episode for tonight' or 'Don't forget you have homework to finish after dinner' can be the difference between a tantrum and success.

Spell it out. Offer choices. Provide a heads-up.

Give Like a Grandparent: Be Nice About It, Provide Freebies and Catch Them Being Good

Close your eyes and conjure up the Quintessential Grandparent, in all their forms.

Some of your fondest memories may be of the fun times eating your Nana's baking, helping your Bubbie make chicken soup or watching a ball game with your Poppa. There is something magical about time spent with grandparents. They give so much of themselves and they ask for so little in return. When they do ask for something, grandchildren typically hop to it without question. This is what this section is all about — giving like that grandparent.

Be nice about it

Let's face it, being the 'taskmaster' is part of the parenting job description. Remember the have-tos? Go to school. Pack your lunch. Brush your teeth. Put on your pyjamas. Come home on time. The list goes on.

1. SETTING THE STAGE

We are not always able to change the number of things our children *have* to do, but we can choose the kind of taskmaster we want to be. Are we a Drill Sergeant barking orders? Or are we the Coach on Team Kid helping them to get the job done?

While the job still gets done, remember to be like the grandparent. Be polite, flexible and understanding.

If your child is in the middle of a game when you ask them to come and set the table, think about whether it would be okay to give them five minutes to finish what they are doing. If your child wants to listen to music or a podcast while they fold the laundry, think about the greater good (the laundry getting folded) rather than the cloying voice of the latest YouTuber or the ridiculously loud cacophony of current hits.

Provide freebies

Throughout the day, find opportunities to provide your child with certain extras and freebies. 'Freebies' refers to items or privileges your children do not have to do anything for and are not expecting. They are just out of the blue. This makes everyone feel good. You will feel better being a 'giver' and your child will certainly feel better as the 'getter'.

> **SCIENCE SIDEBAR**
>
> In geeky behavioural terms, the **Prepare** strategy of being a frequent giver is also known as 'Pairing'. Essentially, the goal is to pair or associate yourself with positive experiences.

This might look like giving an extra ten minutes to play another round of cards, giving extra hugs and kisses, playing catch, giving them that first fresh-out-of-the-oven cookie, letting them watch an extra episode of their favourite show or preparing their favourite side dish with dinner. Essentially, you want to give like that grandparent.

We know there is never, ever enough time in the day. Yet, we cannot emphasize enough just how crucial it is to regularly invest the time. Spend Quality Time with your children. This idea is so important that we have dedicated the entire next chapter to it! When kids feel connected and pair you with positives they will be much more likely to co-operate with your requests.

Catch them being good

Your child is already doing many appropriate and good things. Find opportunities to celebrate those successes, appreciate them for who they are and give them praise for their day-to-day good deeds. Whether your child is sharing with their sibling, turning off the tablet, setting the table or doing their homework, make sure to celebrate the little things. Especially when they are doing tasks spontaneously, with little fuss and without first making a deal.

Life can get very hectic, and it is often overlooked when children are being quiet, helpful or doing what was asked. We suggest *catching them being good* whenever you can.

1. SETTING THE STAGE

CAN YOU RELATE?

Your toddler is playing quietly for ten minutes while you make dinner.

Your child has been working on their homework for a solid twenty minutes.

Not only does your pre-teen spend 30 minutes shovelling snow, but they also clean off your car, knowing you have a meeting to get to.

Our message here is to not take these situations for granted! Notice the good stuff. Be grateful for the small, good things your child does every day. Keep the interactions positive. Get down on the floor with your toddler and move some cars for one minute. Or give praise while they are playing quietly with their cars, *before* they begin screaming for you to come and play. Congratulate the child who has been doing their homework for twenty minutes. They have been working hard, so bring them a snack *before* they have the chance to get distracted. Make a hot chocolate for the pre-teen who has gone the extra mile to clean off your car.

The more you can catch the kids being good, the more they will continue to do it!

Be nice about it. Provide freebies.
Catch them being good.

Putting it Together

Let's review the scenarios presented at the beginning of this chapter. How can the bath avoiding, homework battling, vegetable refusing and Netflix bingeing have had better endings by using the **Prepare** strategies discussed in this chapter?

> Penelope's mother is tired after her hectic day at the office. Tonight is technically bath night, but Mum does not feel she has the energy to fight with Penelope to pull her away from playing with her toys and get her into the tub. Penelope's mum decides to forego bath night (she *picks her battles*), knowing she will be better prepared to handle it tomorrow. She makes a mental note to remind Penelope as soon as she gets home from school tomorrow that she will have a bath (she *gives a heads-up*). She will start the bath process a few minutes earlier than normal (she is *realistic* about how long the transition will take) and she will provide a five-minute warning as bathtime approaches (she gives another *heads-up*). She may even let Penelope bring her favourite toys into the tub with her (she is *nice about it*). The keys to making this a successful transition tomorrow will be for Mum to **pick her battles, give a heads-up** and **be nice about it**.
>
> Joseph's father offers to help with homework. Things are going very well as they work on adding fractions, but Dad knows Joseph does not yet understand how to multiply

fractions. When they move on to this topic, Dad tells Joseph they will only practise three questions tonight (he is *realistic*) and tomorrow night they will do six questions (he *gives a heads-up* and *spells it out*). Joseph grumbles about the work being too hard. Dad reminds him they will do the questions together and asks Joseph if he wants to use popcorn or chocolate chips to visually demonstrate the math concepts (he *gives choices*). Joseph gets the three questions completed, which is fewer than what was assigned, but Joseph and his dad are satisfied that he has learned something and that he will be ready to tackle more questions tomorrow. They enjoy the rest of the popcorn and chocolate chips as they read Joseph's favourite book together. The keys to encouraging Joseph to work on difficult tasks were to **be realistic,** to **spell it out** and **give choices**.

Claude's mother knows her kids do not like to eat their vegetables (she is being *realistic*). So, instead of presenting plates loaded with broccoli, she sets out a veggie appetizer tray they can pick from while they finish their homework (she *offers them a choice* of vegetables to eat). The kids eat all the carrots and red peppers without complaint and when they come to the table for dinner they are excited to see just meat and rice on their plates. Mum feels satisfied knowing her kids ate a healthy snack, even if they did not have vegetables with their dinners. She is so pleased that she gives them each a scoop of gelato for dessert while thanking them for making mealtime pleasant (she *catches her kids being good* at dinner). In this situation, the keys to Mum's success were **being realistic, offering choices** and **catching her kids being good.**

Anjali is told she can watch one episode of her favourite show after dinner (they *spelled out* how much TV she can watch). Her parents know they have to monitor her because Anjali is known for sneaking in extra episodes if they are not paying attention. So her parents decide to watch the show with Anjali, even though it is not very interesting for them (they are *being realistic* about her ability to turn off the TV after only one show). They also brought yogurt and fruit for the family to enjoy (they provide *freebies*). When the show is over and they turn off the TV, they talk with Anjali about the funny things that happened and pretend they really liked it (they are *being nice about it* while they transition away from TV time). Anjali makes no complaint as they move into the bedtime routine. She feels connected to her parents. The evening was a success because her parents **spelled it out**, they were **realistic**, they **provided freebies** and they were **nice about** the transition to bedtime.

1. SETTING THE STAGE

As can be seen from the examples above, these strategies are connected, complementary and work together. They grow from the common purpose of Setting the Stage.

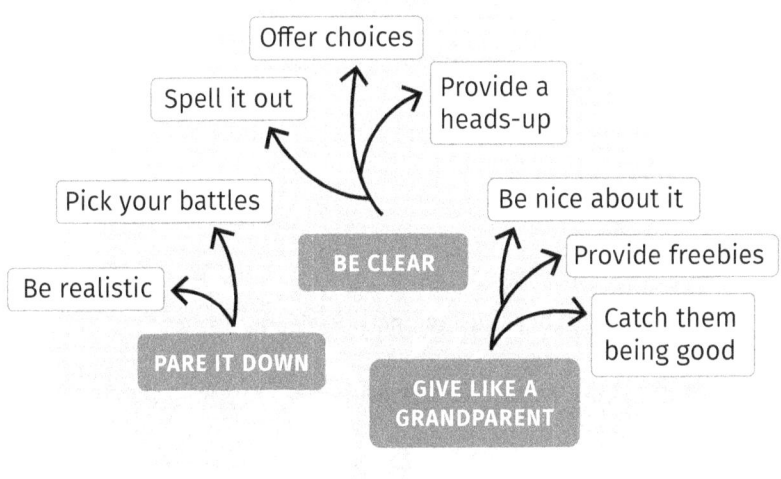

SETTING THE STAGE

The possibilities and combinations are endless, unique to each child and scenario. What *is* fundamental is to **Prepare** your child for success.

PUTTING IT INTO PRACTICE

Now would be the perfect time to take out a pencil and your Parenting Journal and put some of these new skills into practice! Take some time to consider how prepared you were in the past week. Reflect on some times that you were able to Pare it Down, Be Clear or Give like a Grandparent. Record some notes on if and when you were able to **Prepare** in these areas:

Pare it Down

I kept my expectations realistic this week.

I adjusted my expectation(s) this week, and chose a battle *not* to pick.

Be Clear

I described clearly what I expected my child to do.

I gave my child a choice between two items/activities.

I gave them a choice of which they would like to do first.

I provided my child a clear heads-up before they had to stop doing something fun.

Give Like a Grandparent

I gave them a few freebies this week.

We did a fun activity of their choosing this week.

I provided some praise for something they did and I would like to see more of.

2.

Quality Time:
A powerful PREPARE strategy

Let's face it, while we love our kids, and love the idea of spending Quality Time with our happy families, at the end of our busy days, in reality we are tired. Our families are tired.

The mad dash from the end of the work day to bedtime is, for so many families (ours included), the most stressful and conflict-laden time of day. Kids and parents are for the most part working at cross purposes.

Let us explain. As parents, at the end of the day we *actively pursue* getting our 'have tos' done quickly and efficiently. Dinner on the table. Check. Table cleared and kitchen cleaned. Check. Homework done. Check. Kids to bed. Double check. The list goes on.

At the exact same time, our kids *actively avoid* getting their 'have tos' done. Homework. Not now. Chores. It's not fair. Baths. What? It is the time when everyone's energy, patience and goodwill are likely to be hitting rock bottom.

At the end of the day, the last thing we want is to have some self-proclaimed parenting guru telling us that we need to spend Quality Time with our kids. It's like being told that all the time you spend doing their laundry, cooking their food and wiping their butts doesn't earn you Parent of the Year.

We are told, shown and 'coached' that to be the Good Parent we have to enjoy it too! We are here to say 'NO, YOU DON'T'. You do not have to like doing the laundry. You do not have to like helping with homework. You do not have to like wiping their butts.

Quality Time

We are here to suggest a new way to do 'Quality Time'. In this chapter we explain why Quality Time is important for your kids' wellbeing. And the best part is that providing it can lead to more co-operation from your kids!

Then, maybe, just maybe, you might even begin to enjoy that mad dash to bedtime ...

> **CAN YOU RELATE?**
>
> Kids have an uncanny 'spidey-sense' for when we have the least amount of energy, the least amount of time and when we are the most preoccupied. This does not stop them from wanting our attention. It actually seems to make them work overtime to get it.

2. QUALITY TIME

When parents are not giving attention willingly, children can be pretty insistent on getting attention any which way they can, and they may do almost anything to get it. Enter in all those negative behaviours you would rather not have to deal with when you are knee-deep in laundry, dishes or dusting — endless interrupting, picking a fight with a sibling, letting the dog run loose in the neighbourhood, colouring on the walls, flooding the bathtub, emptying the cereal box on the floor ...

RESULT: We end up REACTING to these emergencies and often feel overwhelmed and frustrated by the amount of supervision and attention our kids need.

Prepare

This is where and when Quality Time fits in. It is a powerful and effective *proactive* strategy to set kids up for success and lay the groundwork for co-operation. Quality Time sits squarely in **Prepare**.

It is an *antecedent* strategy used to *prevent* negative behaviour. It is used to increase the co-operative behaviours you want to see later on. It is a 'Before It's Too Late' strategy used to get ahead of the annoying and off-limits behaviours our kids invariably use to try to get our attention.

> **SCIENCE SIDEBAR**
>
> In geeky behaviour lingo 'Quality Time' is also called 'Non-Contingent Reinforcement'.
>
> It is *non-contingent* because the Quality Time you are providing is not tied to, or dependent on, your kids having to do anything for it. They do not have to 'work for', 'earn' it or do anything in particular to get it or to keep it going.
>
> The *reinforcement* part is the uninterrupted *attention* they get from you.

Quality Time: What is it?

Let us begin by clarifying what *we* mean by Quality Time.

Quality Time is spending a designated amount of time with your child (or each child separately) doing something **they** enjoy. Ideally, the activity is something of **their** choosing and it is something you **do together**.

Many parents already use Quality Time regularly, not realizing it is helping to build a strong relationship with their child and increasing their child's co-operation.

2. QUALITY TIME

CAN YOU RELATE?

Derek loves to play basketball. Although his mother is not exactly NBA-level, she spends fifteen minutes after school each day shooting hoops with Derek.

Antonia is obsessed with dinosaurs. Every evening when her dad gets home from work, he spends ten minutes looking through dinosaur books with her, discussing their favourites and imagining what it would be like to see one in real life.

Selina wants a mural on her bedroom wall. Every day Selina and her dad spend at least a bit of time imagining it, drawing it out and purchasing the materials. Then they spend a few weekends actually working on it and bringing their ideas to fruition.

Quality Time: What it's not

Quality Time is about spending time together, doing something that is **not** chores, **not** homework, **not** demanding, **not** screaming, **not** fighting and **not** any of the other not-so-lovely parts of being a parent and being a kid.

Why Should I Bother?

So what's in it for your child?

Uninterrupted parent time — a hot commodity in most families.

What does this do?

For some children it serves to fill their tank and replenish their resources. It gives them some moments of closeness to connect with the most trusted, valued person/people in their life. For other children, it serves to give them a time of complete control over you. They get control over their time and over their life, if only briefly. A time for them to be able to decide after a day at school where they were told what to learn, when to eat and when/what to play. A time before an evening of many demands — having to set the table, having to eat dinner, having to do homework, having to go to bed. It demonstrates your willingness to be open, your trust in them, your commitment to them, your investment in them. It demonstrates your unconditional love and your enjoyment of them.

So what's in it for you?

You have just gained some good will, put money in the bank and set the stage for success.

By filling your child's tank *before* you ask them for anything, they are more likely to have something to give back in terms of co-operation when they are asked to participate in the necessary 'mad dash' tasks of the evening.

SCIENCE SIDEBAR

In fact, there is research to suggest that daily Quality Time, when defined like this, for just ten minutes a day, right after school but before the 'have tos' begin, increases co-operation for the rest of the evening. And wouldn't we all love that!

2. QUALITY TIME

> The advantages of Quality Time are especially important for children who have a harder time with co-operation, who have learning or behavioural difficulties or who have experienced loss or disruption.

There is also always a chance you will re-discover what lovely, funny, interesting kids you have. When you are not asking them to do the endless list of 'have tos' to get through our busy family lives, you can truly have fun together. Enjoy!

Putting the 'Quality' in Quality Time: Essential ingredients

Quality Time has five essential ingredients:

1. *Your child is in the lead and in control.* Ideally, the activity you do with your child during Quality Time is chosen by your child. Remember, the goal is to make yourself 100 per cent available to your child and to fill their need for your attention willingly and happily. That means no cell phone, no email, no making dinner.
2. *A short amount of time is set aside.* Ten to fifteen minutes of uninterrupted Quality Time is ideal. Remember it is *Quality Time*, not *quantity time*. True Quality Time is actually hard to sustain. Any longer than about fifteen minutes and it starts to be a set-up for things to fall apart. Think tantrums, tears and time-outs. In reality, it is a lot easier to find ten minutes in

your day than it is to carve away hours of Quality Time while life awaits, remembering you still have to do the laundry and walk the dogs.

3. *It happens on a regular and consistent basis.* Every attempt should be made to do it every day (or every weekday) and to do it around the same time of day. After they get home from school or you get home from work is optimal. It is a time to 'fill your child's cup' and connect with them before the mad dash to bedtime begins. It is a time to put some 'money in the bank' for when you really do need their co-operation later in the evening.

4. *It is unconditional and non-contingent.* Quality Time happens because it happens. Period. It does not get taken away because seven-year-old Jean got in trouble at school, twelve-year-old Tanisha took a swing at her brother, or four-year-old Sebastian had a meltdown in the grocery store. It does not go by the wayside because you had a lousy day, because you had to fire an employee or because you got yelled at by your boss. It happens because it happens.

5. *You make no requests during the activities/time.* This is an important one and worth repeating: Make no requests. Drop any ideas of turning the activity into a 'teachable moment' or a learning activity. Have no expectations for activities to be completed, skills to be learned, corrected or practised, or games to be played by your rules. You are not in charge. Enjoy it! You have one job to do. One job. Truly follow their lead.

2. QUALITY TIME

And don't worry because it is only ten to fifteen minutes (see #2). Have fun and enjoy it.

Getting Started: The how tos of Quality Time

Make a plan! Define the parameters. Get specific. Write it down. Commit.

PUTTING IT INTO PRACTICE

It's time to take out a pen and your Parenting Journal to begin planning your Quality Time. Here are some considerations and things you will want to make notes of. We've broken it down into manageable steps.

Step 1: When? Pick a time of day. Mark it on a family calendar.

Step 2: How long? Set an amount of time. We recommend ten to fifteen minutes. If this is not realistic for your family, start with a shorter amount of time. Even three minutes spent shooting the breeze with your uncommunicative and 'grunty' pre-teen is time well spent.

Step 3: Where? Pick a location. Or better yet have your child pick a location. This can be flexible and change depending on the activity. You can even go to where your child is in that moment — if they are already having fun doing something.

Step 4: What? Have your child pick something to do during 'their' time. You can spend some time writing down your child's ideas and keep a running list. If your child is at a loss for ideas, feel free to make suggestions. Just be sure to stay flexible. Do not get too invested in your own ideas. It does not matter how much fun *you* think your activity will be. It does not matter how much *you* think your child will enjoy it. If your child is already having fun, join in!

Step 5: With whom? If more than one adult is available you may have some flexibility. Decide if the adults will alternate. Decide if the choice of adult will shift based on the preferred activity. Decide if the choice of activity will shift based on who is available. Decide if your child is permitted to choose with whom they spend their Quality Time on any given day.

You are probably wondering 'How do I know if I'm doing this right?' We have noticed a few things in our clinical practices and when applying this effectively with thousands of families. These unconditional and positive interactions result in a stronger relationship between parents and their children. So much so that children look forward to these times and find ways to involve their parents more and more. This might look like more frequent conversations, more co-operation and kids just wanting to spend more time with their parents.

Be patient. Persist. If you lose your cool, try again ...

Tips and Troubleshooting

The DOs and DON'Ts

» DON'T assume what your child will find fun, interesting or motivating.
» DO ask your child what they want to do.

» DON'T impose your expectations on the activity. For example, what the art project should be, that directions for building Lego are followed as written, that everyone plays a game by the rules. This is a good time to distinguish between playing by 'Maddy's rules' during 'Maddy's time' versus playing by 'Family Rules' at other times.
» DO make suggestions, when they are welcomed.

» DON'T force your child to 'finish' the activity if they do not want to.
» DO be flexible about how it goes, how it turns out and what gets 'accomplished'. Allow room for things to change.

The What Ifs ...

1. 'My child says she does not want to spend time with me.'
    › Your child may be saying this because she may be anticipating that you will not be interested in what she wants to do, that

you will not agree to do what she wants to do, or that you will try to change, teach or correct her during the activity. Try to meet your child where they are and show interest in whatever they want to do or whatever they are into in the moment.
- ⟩ Don't give up. Keep trying to engage and entice your child. Keep letting her know your attention is available and unconditional.

2. 'All my son wants to do is play his *&%$# video games.'
   - ⟩ While it is not ideal, if the ONLY thing your child can come up with is a video game, show an interest in the game, try to understand it and appreciate why they like it.
   - ⟩ Ask your child to explain how the game goes or what they like about it (only if they don't see this as a demand and see it as fun to talk about).
   - ⟩ You can try playing the game together, watching your son play it on his own or just listening to them describe it in detail.
   - ⟩ If your son has your undivided attention, he will know that you care about his interests (even if you really do not care about the many intricacies of Minecraft, Fortnite or whatever the latest obsession is!)

3. 'My son is really controlling.' 'My daughter is so bossy that she wants to tell me exactly what to say and what to do when

we play.' 'All my child wants to do is cheat in the game they chose to play.'

- › Make it clear that all this is okay during 'their time'. You will need to bite your lip, get cheated on, be bossed around.
- › The next time they want to play that game during Quality Time, clarify if they want to play by 'their rules' or 'family rules', just so you know what to do. Remember, it is their choice.

4. 'It's not fair to my other children.' 'My younger son wants to be included in his brother's Quality Time.'
   - › The goal is for each child to have separate time with you that is theirs and theirs alone. Do not double up or suggest you do a group activity.
   - › Try to set up your other child with an activity they can do independently for ten minutes with the promise they will get their Quality Time next, or the next day (alternate days) or when their younger siblings go to bed.
   - › If it is a two-adult situation, perhaps the other adult can occupy the sibling. Only include siblings if it is okay with the child whose Quality Time it is supposed to be.

5. 'I can't stand the activity my child chose!'
   - › The short answer: Suck it up, Buttercup!
   - › Alternatively, you could throw the other adult under the bus and suggest the child save it for a time when the other parent is available for Quality Time. ☺

6. 'My daughter's ideas are completely ridiculous! We cannot build a roller coaster in the backyard!'
   - You are right — you cannot build a real roller coaster in the backyard. But you *can* imagine it together, draw it together or do research on roller coasters together. Maybe an obstacle course will feel like a reasonable substitute for your daughter.
   - Try to support your children's creativity and imagination. Avoid shutting them down or telling them their ideas are impossible.
   - Indulge them during Quality Time!

7. 'My child can't think of anything she wants to do.'
   - Remember, it is okay to suggest activities, games, topics for discussion. It is okay to suggest you look online for ideas. It is just *not okay* to impose your ideas or make them stick with something if they don't want to continue.

SECTION II

—

Teach

3.

Being a 'Skills Detective'

Parents are teachers. Apart from tending to our children's basic needs, such as feeding, clothing and bathing, most of parenting is actually teaching. We teach our children new things all the time. From the moment our babies enter the world, we are teaching them to play with us, to imitate us, to look at us when we call their name, to communicate with us and to trust us.

It is probably safe to say that the ultimate parenting goal is to raise humans who are happy and independent. There are many skills we need to teach our children in order to raise them to be resilient, confident and likeable.

In most situations, the goals of our teaching are very obvious. For example, when we teach children how to brush their teeth, it is because we want them to learn how to brush their teeth thoroughly and independently. Or when we teach them how to fold the laundry,

3. BEING A 'SKILLS DETECTIVE'

it is because we want them to actually be able to fold the laundry properly. Pretty straightforward, right?

However, sometimes children need to be taught skills that are not quite as evident. For a child who seems to ignore their parents every time an instruction is given, they may actually need to be taught how to co-operate. Another child may benefit from explicit teaching on how to wait their turn. And yet another may need to learn how to express their emotions in ways that do not hurt themselves, other people or property.

CAN YOU RELATE?

Ten-year-old Anahita is asked to tidy her room. She agrees to do so, but an hour later the job is not done.

RESULT: Anahita's parents are angry with her and see her as lazy and ungrateful.

Young Alejandro asks if he can have ice cream. His father tells him 'no'. Alejandro cries, kicks and yells for the next twenty minutes.

RESULT: Alejandro's father feels frustrated and thinks his son is spoiled.

William's mother is in the middle of an important Zoom meeting. William interrupts her several times to ask questions, to show his Lego set and to complain about his sister. He continues to interrupt even when he is threatened with the removal of all media for the rest of the day.

RESULT: William's mother is exhausted with his behaviour and worries that he is selfish, impulsive and too needy.

We believe that all problem behaviour arises because a child is missing a skill or is attempting to communicate something. We do not think of children as 'bad', 'lazy', 'disobedient' or 'spoiled'. Rather, **Prepare. Teach. Motivate.** starts with the assumption that all children have the desire to do well. Whether your child is 'spirited', 'deeply feeling', 'highly sensitive' or downright disagreeable, we strongly believe they truly want to avoid problems. They would prefer to get along with their parents. They want to be happy. They want you to be happy. They want you to be happy with them. But, sometimes, children lack specific skills that would help them reach these goals.

SCIENCE SIDEBAR

A well-known, scientifically supported way of understanding and treating disruptive behaviour called 'Collaborative and Proactive Solutions' is based on the premise that 'Kids do well if they can' (www.livesinthebalance.org). This means children have the desire to be co-operative and pleasant, but when the expectation being placed on them exceeds their abilities,

> problem behaviour results. They are lacking the *skill* to do well, not the *will* to do well.
>
> This view of children and youth wanting to do well is dramatically different from seeing challenging kids as attention-seeking, defiant, manipulative or poorly motivated. Research has shown that assuming the best of kids and teaching them the skills they need is a highly effective approach, even for those with extremely challenging, even dangerous, behaviours.

Before we can jump into teaching our children new skills, we must carefully determine what skill(s) they are missing, or what they are trying to communicate. In this chapter, we will help parents identify missing skills, and related teachable goals, for any challenging situation they encounter. We want all parents to be 'skill detectives'! This is an easy yet powerful parenting technique that simply requires parents to understand that unwanted, challenging behaviours stem from a lack of skill(s).

Collecting Information

The first task for any good detective is to collect information. Often, the easiest way to start is to identify the things you *do not want* your child to do anymore.

Let's go back to the earlier examples…

> **CAN YOU RELATE?**
>
> Ten-year-old Anahita is asked to tidy her room. She agrees to do so, but an hour later the job is not done. Parents *do not want* Anahita to procrastinate about cleaning her room.
>
> Young Alejandro asks if he can have ice cream. His father tells him 'no'. Alejandro cries, kicks and yells for the next twenty minutes. Alejandro's father *does not want* him to have a tantrum when he is told no.
>
> William's mother is in the middle of an important Zoom meeting. William interrupts her several times to ask questions, to show his Lego set and to complain about his sister. He continues to interrupt even when he is threatened with the removal of all media for the rest of the day. William's mother *does not want* him to interrupt her when she is in a meeting.

Finding the Positive Opposite

It is generally quite easy to figure out what we do not want our children to do. The next step, which is sometimes a bit more difficult, is to determine what we wish our children would do instead. If you were a fly on the wall in the situation, what would your child be doing if they were 'doing it right'? This is sometimes referred to as finding an alternative or 'replacement' to the problem behaviour. In essence, we want to identify the Positive Opposite.

3. BEING A 'SKILLS DETECTIVE'

> **SCIENCE SIDEBAR**
>
> The technique of teaching the Positive Opposite is well researched.
>
> Behaviour scientists have found it works much better than punishing a behaviour we do not want to see. This is because children do not just need to learn what *not* to do, but they also have to learn what they *should* do.
>
> Although it is tempting to use punishment to get rid of problem behaviour, using it alone will not lead to permanent change. The research on this is very clear. Please refer to Chapter 6, 'Understanding Punishment', for an in-depth discussion of this phenomenon.

Practically speaking, it is very difficult to teach someone to *not* do something. We tend to teach people to do something.

If we want our children to stop falling off their bicycle, we need to teach them to ride it. If we want our children to stop pooping in their diapers, we need to teach them to poop in the toilet. If we want our children to stop being rude when they speak to us, we need to teach them to be polite. Instead of teaching our children to stop leaving dirty clothes on the floor, we need to teach them to put their dirty clothes in the hamper.

Again, let's return to our examples...

CAN YOU RELATE?

Ten-year-old Anahita is asked to tidy her room. She agrees to do so, but an hour later the job is not done.

POSITIVE OPPOSITE: Anahita cleans her room as soon as she is asked.

Young Alejandro asks if he can have ice cream. His father tells him 'no'. Alejandro cries, kicks and yells for the next twenty minutes.

POSITIVE OPPOSITE: Alejandro expresses his disappointment and accepts that he is not able to have the ice cream.

William's mother is in the middle of an important Zoom meeting. William interrupts her several times to ask questions, to show his Lego set and to complain about his sister. He continues to interrupt even when he is threatened with the removal of all media for the rest of the day.

POSITIVE OPPOSITE: William amuses himself quietly while his mother is taking a work call.

Digging Deeper

Now that you have identified the Positive Opposite, or what you want your child to do, the next step is to dig a little deeper and determine what is preventing your child from doing what you want. Can you identify barriers that may be stopping your child from actually doing the Positive Opposite?

Getting back to Anahita and her messy room. Her parents have clearly identified the goal of having her clean her room as soon as she has been asked. So what is actually preventing her from doing so?

» Is she overwhelmed by the task? Does she not know how to get started?

» Is she exhausted from her day at school?

» Is she distracted by her favourite YouTuber?

» Does she not realize how much time has passed since her parents asked her to clean her room?

» Is she being defiant? Does she have frequent difficulty co-operating with many of her parents' requests?

In some cases, there are no skills to teach. The challenge may be a one-off situation. Maybe you can address the situation with **Prepare** strategies only.

In other situations, your child may need to learn a new skill in order to be successful. Knowing the barrier allows a good detective to be specific in terms of honing in on what is missing. For Anahita, some possible **Prepare** and **Teach** solutions may include the following:

- » Anahita may need to learn to ask for help to clean her room, to get started and/or to break down the task into manageable steps.
- » Knowing that Anahita is exhausted after school, parents could 'set the stage' and only ask her to do chores on the weekends.
- » Anahita may need to learn how to transition away from YouTube when asked.
- » Anahita may need to learn to use a timer or refer to a clock to help her manage her time appropriately.
- » Anahita may need to learn to be more co-operative in general to her parents' requests.

Let's continue to dig a little deeper into why Alejandro may have had such a hard time when his dad refused him ice cream and why William was so incessantly interrupting his mother during her call.

For Alejandro, let's consider some possible barriers for him to more appropriately express his disappointment with not getting ice cream.

- » Is he tired after his day at preschool?
- » Is he overheated on a hot summer day?
- » Did he not have his lunch that day and is hungry?
- » Was he promised an ice cream if he had a good day at school?
- » Does he often have tantrums when he is told he cannot have something?
- » Does he know how to express his frustration in other ways?

3. BEING A 'SKILLS DETECTIVE'

Selecting the skills to teach (or not teach) Alejandro will depend on which is the most likely barrier:

- » If he is hungry, tired or overheated, it is unlikely there is a skill to teach a preschooler. But it is important to recognize these signs and ensure those needs are met by providing snacks or cool beverages. Our 'Setting the Stage' chapter will help **Prepare** your child in the future for these scenarios.
- » If he is not eating his lunch at preschool, consider some reasons why he may not be. Are there foods he does not like? Is he not able to open the containers or ask for help?
- » If you had promised him an ice cream for a good day at school, as a parent you must follow through with that deal. If Alejandro did have a good day, he should get an ice cream. If he did not have a good day, he does not earn the ice cream and you may need to wait out the tantrum that comes as a result. That said, you may want to skip ahead to the chapter 'Understanding Reinforcement' to better understand how to use rewards effectively to **Motivate** children, after which you may reconsider offering an ice cream for a good day at preschool. It might also be helpful to review the 'Setting the Stage' chapter to set realistic expectations for children's behaviour, where you will likely realize that it may not be reasonable to expect a preschooler to have an entirely good day.
- » Alejandro might need to learn to tolerate being told no.
- » Alejandro could learn better ways to express his frustration.

And finally, for William, the interrupter. Possible barriers preventing him from achieving his mother's goal of amusing himself quietly while she is on a work call could include the following:

- » Is he able to play independently?
- » Are the activities of interest to him?
- » Has Mum had a busy work-day and had fewer interactions with William?
- » Does William consistently require a lot of attention from his mother or other adults?
- » If he is expected to be working on homework or school activities, is he able to do the work? Is he able to do it independently?
- » Do William and his sister have difficulties getting along?
- » Does William often have difficulty waiting for things?

Again, some of these barriers would not require skills to be taught. Identifying the correct barrier is key to deciding whether to use a **Prepare** or a **Teach** strategy to improve William's skills:

- » Developing independent play skills might be a teaching/learning goal.
- » William's mother may need to 'set the stage' by selecting some activities with William that might be of interest to him, before the next meeting.
- » Hectic days can be a challenge. His mother may need to 'set the stage' by planning to periodically spend some 'Quality Time', even if only briefly, between meetings. This can make a big difference.

3. BEING A 'SKILLS DETECTIVE'

» William may need to learn a better way to get Mum's attention without interrupting her meeting.
» His mother may want to 'set the stage' by keeping the difficult school work tasks for when she is available to help William.
» William and his sister may need to learn how to get along better.
» William may need to learn the underlying skill of waiting.

As you can see from the above examples, some of the possible barriers are obvious and others less so. Through the process of 'digging deeper' and allowing yourself to think about why your child may really be behaving the way they are, you may discover opportunities to better set them up for success. Or you may find previously undetected missing skills that need to be taught.

Looking for Themes or Underlying Skill Deficits

Once you have identified the Positive Opposite in a few situations, the next step for the 'Skills Detective' is to look for any underlying themes in their child's behaviour. For example, Anahita's parents may realize that she tends to procrastinate with many of the requests that they make. She is slow to get ready for school, she often doodles when she should be doing her homework and she is late for bed most of the time because it takes her a long time to complete the bedtime routine.

For Alejandro, his detective parents may realize that he has tantrums at other times as well. Not only does he tantrum when he cannot have an ice cream, but he also tantrums when his parents turn off the TV and when his brother does not let Alejandro play with him. Once they have collected the information, identified the Positive Opposites and dug into underlying reasons for his behaviour, it is clear that Alejandro is lacking the skill of tolerating being told 'no' or 'not right now'.

Not all situations will have an underlying theme. Sometimes children need to work on a single skill (e.g., brushing their teeth). But, we have found that children often have a foundational skill deficit that shows itself in multiple situations. While it may look like your child has many different problems, in some cases it is just one bigger problem that happens across contexts.

Common themes or broader underlying skill deficits include:

» difficulties communicating their emotions in a functional/acceptable way
» difficulties waiting patiently
» difficulties accepting when told 'no' or 'not right now'
» difficulties co-operating
» difficulties turning off a screen (phone, TV, tablet, etc.)
» difficulties doing routine tasks independently and on time.

If during your 'Skills Detective' work you discover that your child is lacking one of the above foundational skills, please refer to Chapters 7 to 12 in this book for detailed discussions on how to teach them. We have found these themes to be so common that we have dedicated entire chapters to each one.

3. BEING A 'SKILLS DETECTIVE'

Reality Check

Great work, Detectives! The last step before moving on to teaching your child the skill(s) they are missing is to conduct a quick, but crucial, reality check. This involves answering the following questions:

1. *Is my child ready to learn this new skill?* Consider your child's age, maturity level and willingness to learn. While it might not be reasonable for a four year old to be able to fold their clothing, it is probably realistic for a ten year old. Still, not all ten year olds have the patience, dexterity or willingness to do such a job on their own. Be realistic with your expectations for your child. Keep in mind that every child is unique and will move forward at their own pace. Just because your sister's daughter is very independent, it does not mean your same-age daughter is capable of the same thing.

2. *Am I ready to teach?* This is a very important question and it pays to be honest with yourself. Consider how much time and energy you have to devote to teaching your child a new skill. If you have just started a new job, or you're about to move to a new home, or you are caring for a parent, or there is a new baby in the house (and the list of possible reasons goes on!), teaching may not be feasible at the moment. That is okay. Let us repeat — that is okay. Wait until you and/or your parenting partner has adequate time and energy to put into teaching. It is much better to wait until you are ready than to start something that you cannot complete.

3. *Of the skills I have identified, which one is the top priority?* Although most children have many things they could be learning, they will be most successful when they are learning only one new skill at a time. This is especially true if they are working on one of the foundational skills, such as co-operation, tolerating no, etc., which tend to take more effort and time.

Being a 'Skills Detective' will help you shift your thinking and your paradigm. It will help you to be more positive and productive while parenting in even the most frustrating and challenging situations. Since this is a new way of thinking, becoming a 'Skills Detective' will get easier with practice ...

> **PUTTING IT INTO PRACTICE**
>
> To guide you in honing your 'Skills Detective' strategies, we've broken it into easy-to-follow steps. Write this in your Parenting Journal to determine what skills your child may need to develop.
>
> Step 1: Select one thing that you want your child to stop doing. Try to be as specific as possible (e.g., location, people present, time of day, etc.).
>
> Step 2: Write down what you want your child to do instead. In other words, what is the Positive Opposite?

3. BEING A 'SKILLS DETECTIVE'

Step 3: Dig deeper. What are some possible barriers to your child achieving the Positive Opposite? Think of at least three barriers. Circle the one that is the most likely barrier.

Step 4: For the barrier you have selected, is this a **Prepare** or a **Teach** situation, or BOTH?

> - If it is a **Prepare** situation, how will you 'set the stage' to minimize these barriers and decrease the likelihood of misbehaviour?
> - If it is a **Teach** situation, what is the missing skill you will teach? Is it a specific skill or is it a general underlying skill (i.e., theme)?

Step 5: Reality Check: Is your child ready to learn this new skill? Are you ready to teach them? Is this skill currently a priority?

Once you have identified the skills to teach, you're ready to move on to the next chapter, which will walk you through *how* to **Teach** your child these new skills.

4.

TEACHing

Now that you have become a top-notch 'Skills Detective', you can confidently:

- » identify exactly what you *don't* want to see
- » figure out what the Positive Opposite would be, and
- » dig deeper to discover the barrier that is preventing your child from behaving better.

You are now ready to tackle the next phase — **Teach**. Roll up your sleeves and let's start **Teaching**.

> **SCIENCE SIDEBAR**
>
> In teaching new skills, you have a whole menu of evidence-based strategies and techniques that are well grounded in behavioural science — prompting, shaping, reinforcement,

4. TEACHING

> back-stepping, backward chaining, visual schedules, first-then contingencies and the list goes on …
>
> Many parents use these skills everyday, and they may not even know it!

Before you decide *how* you are going to teach your child a lacking skill, you need to figure out the *when* and the *what* (based on what skill you discovered is lacking when digging deeper in your detective work).

WHEN to TEACH

Remember that when teaching any new skill, your child will need to be in a receptive state — one in which they will be likely to co-operate with the teaching opportunity. Do **Teach** in moments when your child is in 'their happy place'.

Please, do not attempt to **Teach** when your child is highly emotionally dysregulated. If their behaviour has escalated to the point of utter meltdown, crying fit or trashing the room, skip to Chapter 11, 'We Can Handle This Together', for important **Prepare** strategies to set up your child for success.

We want to catch the 'teachable moment' *before* things escalate, or when things are calm. When you see that things may be ramping up, the teaching opportunity has passed you by.

WHAT to TEACH

Once parents have mastered the art of being a 'Skills Detective', they have already determined what skill their child is lacking. The next step is to define that missing skill as a SMART goal. SMART goals are:

- » **S**pecific
- » **M**easurable/observable
- » **A**chievable
- » **R**elevant
- » **T**ime-limited.

> **CAN YOU RELATE?**
>
> Lucy's mother is tired of admonishing her daughter for playing too roughly with the family's cat. Despite frequent reminders to 'play nicely', 'stop manhandling Fluffy' and 'be gentle', Lucy does not change her behaviour. Her mother is exasperated and worried that her daughter has little empathy for how the cat feels.

SMART goal-setting forces us to think carefully about what we want to teach and whether or not it is realistic. SMART goal-setting allows us to prioritize a specific skill to work on and to define it clearly. As good skills detectives, we already know we are looking for the

4. TEACHING

Positive Opposite as a replacement for an undesired behaviour. SMART goal-setting also includes the reality check of whether your child is capable of this new skill and whether it is actually important to their day-to-day functioning, and it ensures we are going to teach the new skill in a timely fashion.

Let's go back to Lucy and her cat to develop a SMART goal …

> **CAN YOU RELATE?**
>
> Lucy's mother decides to teach her daughter to play gently with her cat. Using the SMART framework, Lucy's mother defines the goal as follows:
>
> › **S**pecific — Lucy will learn to stroke the cat softly and hold Fluffy in a gentle grasp.
>
> › **M**easureable — Lucy's mother defines 'softly' as being equivalent pressure to simply resting her hand on the cat. A 'gentle grasp' means that the cat can get away at any time and is not forcibly held in Lucy's arms.
>
> › **A**chievable — Lucy has already learned to be gentle with her baby sister, so it seems reasonable to expect that she can learn to be gentle with Fluffy as well.
>
> › **R**elevant — This is an important goal since Lucy really wants to play with Fluffy but Fluffy often avoids her.

> **T**ime-Limited — Lucy's mother plans to work on this skill for two weeks and will evaluate Lucy's progress along the way, adjusting as needed. If she cannot learn this skill in that time, they will put the teaching on hold until Lucy has matured further.

What you teach generally falls into two categories: Actions and Reactions.

Generally, when our kids are not behaving the way we want or expect, when it comes down to it we either want them to *act* differently or *react* differently.

TEACHing new REACTIONS

Let's deal with teaching new *reactions* first.

Whining. Screaming. Crying. Demanding. Negotiating. Sound familiar?

Reactions that parents often talk to us about wanting to change include their children acting entitled and spoiled/rude, freaking out when they don't get what they want, or melting down when they actually need help doing something.

At the same time, parents talk to us about their worry that if they do not respond to their child with love, empathy, calming by giving in and physical contact, their child will feel unheard, abandoned and broken.

4. TEACHING

Here we describe a warm and compassionate process that both meets your child's emotional needs and your behavioural wants for them, which gets them closer to where they want to be.

Thinking of Positive Opposites, what we would really like them to do is to ask politely, and deal less aggressively with their disappointments so that we can comfort them when they are upset and ask for help when/if they need it.

HOW to TEACH new reactions

Teaching Functional Communication

One of the most important skills for children to learn is to communicate in a constructive and productive manner. We are going to use the skill of Functional Communication to illustrate several different teaching strategies.

> **CAN YOU RELATE?**
>
> Megan is hangry. She shouts at her dad, 'Get me some crackers!' Her dad, frustrated, feels put out and a little hurt by his daughter's rude tone, and lectures her about how he is not her butler, as he prepares her a plate of crackers. Feeling badly for his daughter about how hungry she must be, he adds some cheese and grapes to her plate. Megan looks at the plate, tells her dad how she didn't even want cheese and grapes and gobbles down the crackers without so much as a

> thank you. Her dad is even more exasperated, hurt and angry with her for being self-centred, rejecting and ill-mannered.

Your child's current behaviours (tantrums, crying, whining) are indeed communications. They're communicating undying desire for something, the depth of disappointment and the intensity of frustration when they cannot do something or have not met their own expectations. While this is true — they are communicating the intensity of their feeling in the moment — they are not acting in ways that get them closer to their goals of being understood, of getting what they want, of being soothed when they are upset, or being able to do something to their own satisfaction while maintaining a positive connection with you. They are actually acting in ways that get them *further* from their goals.

While your child's tantrum, meltdown, rude tone or crying are definitely telling us something, they are not actually communicating in an effective and productive way to get what they want or need. And to be sure, when you respond to those types of communications from your children by giving them what they want, negotiating, hugging and cajoling, you are most definitely increasing the likelihood of them using those tactics again when they don't get what they want, when they need a hug or when they need some help. On the other hand, even though you may be angry or exasperated, when you respond with threatening this is 'the last time' or chastise them for being rude or childish while you do it, you are also reinforcing the unwanted way they are communicating. We will discuss the ins and outs of reinforcement in the next chapter.

4. TEACHING

There is a better way. We need to **Teach** it to them. We need to teach them to communicate more functionally — in a way that gets them what they want and in a way that both parties can feel good about. Functional Communication skills let other people know what you need in a clear, direct and (more) calm way that is much more likely to be met with open arms, an open heart and an open mind.

Here is how you **Teach** Functional Communication skills. The main strategies you will use are Prompting, Modelling, Practising, Shaping, Reinforcement and Fading.

Prompting Functional Communication allows you to avoid reinforcing inappropriate requests (such as whining, grunting, demanding) and therefore reduces how often they occur. It teaches the Positive Opposite. Prompting is when you suggest to them they will get what they are after if they ask in a nicer way. Whenever possible, we anticipate what our child may be wanting, and prompt the appropriate request *before* they have the opportunity to grunt or demand it. We call this an antecedent prompt.

Model for them, by giving your child the words you would like them to use, in a tone you would like them to use.

Adding in a strategy called 'practising' ensures your child practises the Positive Opposite behaviour before their request is granted. *Practising* is when you ask your child to 'try it again one more time', using the words you have just given them and with the tone you would like to hear. Finding and creating frequent practice opportunies allows for quicker skill development.

This combination of teaching strategies *shapes* your child's behaviour into what you want to see. When you are first teaching your child to use new phrases with a new tone, recognize that it will be hard for them. Your best approach will be to reward their *best or better effort*, not the perfect one. As your child gets more and more practice, you raise your expectations and reward their attempts that get closer and closer to the end goal. You are gradually *shaping* their skill.

> **CAN YOU RELATE?**
>
> You might remember Juanita and her father from the 'Setting the Stage' chapter. Dad wanted to enjoy a nice, relaxing meal with his family, but Juanita was done eating and talking after fifteen minutes. If Juanita actually has the maturity and patience to sit at the table for 30 minutes, Dad could build her skills by 'shaping' them.
>
> Starting at a level in which Juanita is currently successful (i.e., fifteen minutes at the table), Dad praises her behaviour and excuses her at this time. After three or four days of success at the fifteen-minute stage, Dad then has Juanita stay at the table for twenty minutes before she is praised and excused. After another three or four days, Juanita is sitting for 25 minutes before being praised and excused, and, not long thereafter, she is sitting at the dining table for the full 30 minutes.
>
> Her father successfully shaped how long she sat at the table. Now Dad may want to work on other manners, like having everyone seated before people start to eat.

4. TEACHING

Reinforcement here is key! The fact that your child gets what they want by asking appropriately is the reward and the thing that will motivate them to ask like that again in the future.

As your child gets better and better at using Functional Communication, you start to provide them with fewer prompts and models. This is called '*fading*'.

With this process of Prompting, Modelling, Practising, Shaping, Reinforcement and Fading, your child will learn that it is easier, faster and much more pleasant to use the new Positive Opposite than it is to use the old problematic behaviour.

Here are some examples of how teaching can happen.

> **PUTTING IT INTO PRACTICE**
>
> Listen in on nine-year-old Megan and her dad:
>
> Megan: 'GET ME SOME CRACKERS!'
>
> Dad: 'Can you ask me nicely, please? Try asking like this: "Dad, can I have some crackers, please?"' (This is Prompting and Modelling.)
>
> In time Dad could prompt more generally. Rather than giving Megan the words, he might ask 'Can you think of another way to say that?' Eventually, when Megan asks 'with tone', Dad simply pauses and gives her 'the look' to say, try again. (This is called Fading.)

Megan: 'Jeez, Dad (eye-roll)! Can I have some crackers, please?' (A slightly better request.)

Dad: 'Sure thing. I'll get them for you.' (Reinforcement — Megan gets what she asked for.)

PUTTING IT INTO PRACTICE

Every time the family goes in the car, Megan yells for her favourite playlist to be played on the stereo.

Knowing this, when they get in the car, Dad immediately reminds Megan she can ask nicely for her favourite playlist *before* she has a chance to yell.

Dad: Hey, Megan. I know you like to listen to your playlist. I'm happy to put it on if you ask me nicely. (Antecedent Prompt.)

Megan asks: 'Can we listen to my playlist?' (Appropriate Request.)

Dad: 'For sure', and turns on the playlist. (Reinforcement — Megan gets what she asked for.)

During this period of teaching your child new ways of responding to you, it will be important for you to stop reinforcing the inappropriate requests. This means that instead of responding to all the 'signals' your child sends that they need/want something, you need to wait until they choose to phrase their request more constructively before responding.

As you can see, it takes longer (and takes more effort) for Megan to get her snack when she asks rudely. Soon she will find that her aggressive tone is now inefficient and ineffective. Over time she will begin to spontaneously ask appropriately because it is faster, requires less effort and it feels better not to aggravate her dad.

The best part is that she learned how to ask appropriately without anyone having to scold her, shame her, explain how she made them feel or 'teach her a lesson'.

With these new Functional Communication skills, it is a WIN–WIN. Both parties walk away satisfied and content — your child has got what they need/want and you can feel good about having a 'good parenting moment' rather than feeling like the nag, punisher or scolder.

Teaching Co-operation

Another important and appropriate reaction that we want from our children is co-operation. Teaching co-operation skills ensures that your child actually listens to you and will respond to you with a positive attitude and open mind to learn new skills. This starts with teaching your child to co-operate when you ask them to do something. Luckily we have a whole chapter devoted to teaching your child this fundamentally important skill. Permission to jump ahead to Chapter 7 on 'Teaching co-operation'.

TEACHing new ACTIONS

Now to let's turn our attention to teaching new *actions* — things you want your child to learn to do on their own so you do not always have to do it for them, such as setting the table, emptying the dishwasher, packing their backpack, getting ready to go in the morning or getting ready for bed at night ... the list can get long.

First off, know that you can really only teach one thing at a time. So pick one thing and let the rest go ... for now.

Teaching Routines

Visual Schedules and Checklists. Visual schedules and/or checklists are effective ways to teach new skills (e.g.,setting the table) and new routines (e.g.,bedtime). The 'schedule' or 'checklist' part refers to the mapping out of each step in the routine or task.

It is important that you make sure your child can actually do each step independently. If they cannot, you may need to model the task from start to finish for them (e.g.,show them how to set the table) or teach them one particular step in the task (e.g.,where to put cutlery in the place setting).

The 'visual' element refers to how you present it to them. With younger children, use pictures to represent the steps. With older children, use words. These need not be fancy or require special programs to create pictures. Use whatever you have — sticky notes, scrap paper, pictures from magazines.

You can also use visual schedules and checklists in another way: to map out/chunk out what will happen in a day. Providing your child with information about what you will require them to

4. TEACHING

do throughout the day may decrease their resistance to transitions, planned activities and tasks. Together with your child, you can draw pictures or use words to name the tasks that need to be completed as part of their day.

For example, once you have taught your child each step in the morning/bedtime routine or the steps for success in other portions of the day where there are several things you need them to do (e.g.,after-school routine), your child can decide what they might like when they get that routine done. You can build the schedule with your child. You can encourage your child to cross off or check the tasks once completed.

> **CAN YOU RELATE?**
>
> Levi, a ten year old, walks in the door after school, steps out of his shoes that he leaves in front of the door, takes off his backpack and leaves it in the hallway and his lunch box on the bench. He sloughs off his jacket and leaves it in a heap on the stairs. About twenty minutes later, his mother emerges from her home office to say hi and sees the trail of his things leading to his room. She yells up the stairs, 'Levi, you are driving me nuts!! I've asked you umpteen times to put your stuff away!' She mumbles, 'I am not his maid' as she shoves his sneakers to the side, hangs his jacket and backpack on a hook and takes his lunchbox to the kitchen.

PUTTING IT INTO PRACTICE

Now let's use a visual schedule to **Teach** Levi the after-school routine of putting his things where they go.

Step 1: His mum explains they are going to use a checklist of the things he needs to do when he comes home after school.

Step 2: Levi and his mother decide that when he has successfully used the checklist to put his things away, he will earn ten extra minutes of screen-time. Then, together they make the list in the order he should do them. As they are thinking it through, Levi even suggests a step of emptying his lunchbox of his dirty containers!

Step 3: They hang the checklist in the front foyer so Levi can see it as soon as he walks in the door.

Step 4: Levi comes home from school the next day and sees the checklist. Levi proceeds to put his shoes on the mat out of the doorway, hang up his backpack, take his lunchbox to the kitchen and put his dirty containers in the sink. He tells his mum he is finished and asks if he can access his extra minutes on his phone (as all his apps have parental controls for how much time he is allowed per day). His mum notices he forgot about hanging up his jacket. Not expecting perfection, she decides to remind him to hang up his jacket. She also decides that doing four of five of the actionables on his list will earn him his minutes.

4. TEACHING

Step 5: Levi happily goes to his room to play his game.

The next day, when Levi says he is done, his mother gives him a less direct reminder to check that he has 'done them all' (Prompting). Levi is happy to get his extra minutes of screen time and his mother is happy she does not have to pick up after her son. WIN–WIN.

First – Then. A simplified visual strategy is to use a 'First – Then' set up. This visual strategy is helpful when there is one step, the steps are well established and you would like to develop new habits. It is used when there is something you would like your child to do before they get to do what they want. Some examples for younger children might include 'First eat dinner – Then videos' and 'First brush teeth – Then stories'. For older children, some examples might be 'First take out the rubbish – Then get a snack' or 'First empty the dishwasher – Then get the WiFi code'. These are simply represented with a picture of what you want them to do and an arrow pointing to a picture of what they want to do. For older children, you may want to use a keyword or short phrase rather than pictures. Some children do not require the visual, and you can just tell them that they will 'First walk the dog – Then video games'.

Pick your words carefully. We recommend that you say 'First – Then', rather than 'If – Then' in these situations. Save the 'If – Then' for when you are offering choices and it is acceptable for them to refuse.

Before using 'First – Then' teaching strategies, you again need to make sure your child can independently do the 'first' part. This strategy is helpful when you are sure your child understands what to do, yet may need to see the connection between doing what you want them to do and them doing what they want or getting what they want.

Backward Chaining. The strategy of Backward Chaining is a gradual and gentle way to teach more complex skills or multi-step tasks. First, you need to break down the complex skill or task into a series of simplified one-step actions. From here, the process of Backward Chaining is quite simple. The parent participates by doing all the steps with (and for) the child *until* you reach the last step. For the last step, coach your child to complete it on their own. Don't forget to provide lots of praise, attention and perhaps even a desired activity or object when the task is done.

Once your child easily performs the last step (with minimal coaching, guidance or prompting), ask them to do the last two steps in the chain of actions needed to complete the task. Again, celebrate the smooth completion of the task with your child.

Continue in this fashion until your child is competently and independently completing all the steps to get the job done. Don't forget to keep celebrating until this skill becomes a habit.

A good example to demonstrate Backward Chaining is teaching a complex skill like toothbrushing. While we may take for granted that this is a one-step activity — brush your teeth — it is actually made up of many small steps. So, rather than fighting and arguing about it, or re-doing your child's attempt at brushing their own teeth, here is an example of how to break it down:

Step 1: Wet toothbrush.

Step 2: Uncap toothpaste.

Step 3: Squeeze a pea-size amount of toothpaste onto toothbrush.

Step 4: Brush top teeth on the inside then outside.

Step 5: Brush bottom teeth on the inside then outside.

Step 6: Spit out toothpaste.

Praise and celebrate your child's success.

To backwards chain, help your child complete steps 1–5, and then have your child spit. As they are more successful in doing this, complete steps 1–4 for your child and then have them brush their bottom teeth, then spit. And so on.

Another example is unloading the dishwasher. The parent assists with unloading the dishwasher first, beginning with the bowls, plates and cups, then the child will unload the utensils. As the child becomes more comfortable with unloading the utensils, the parent empties the bowls and plates, and the child then unloads the cups and utensils. Over time, they will be able to empty the dishwasher and put all the dishes away on their own.

Teaching Task Initiation/Starting and Perseverance/Finishing

Prompting. Prompting is the action of saying or doing something to persuade, encourage or remind someone to do something. We saw the use of verbal prompting in the above example of teaching Megan new Functional Communication skills to replace her demanding and whiny tone when asking for something. Her father first gave her the words to use and then faded out his verbal prompt by replacing the exact words with a more general question about trying again. We also saw it with Levi's mum, who reminded him to check the checklist to make sure he got all the steps of the after-school routine done.

Here we will explore the 'doing' side of prompting because, most of the time, we would like our kids to just learn to do something themselves without the reminders that can easily slip into nagging, hounding and begging. There are a couple of ways to use non-verbal prompting: Physical Proximity and Modelling.

Physical proximity can be an effective non-speaking way of supporting your child when you are asking them to do something they often do not start or finish on their own. You are not teaching the skills involved in doing the task, but instead teaching the skill of perseverance, stick-to-it-ive-ness and focus to stay on task.

Task initiation. How close you are to your child when you are asking them to do something has a significant impact on how likely they are to co-operate. So, instead of shouting a request from another room, go to where your child is, get their attention and ask them to complete the job you had in mind.

Task completion. Another circumstance in which you may want to use your physical presence as a reminder is during a task you know they can do but do not necessarily have the stamina or attention to stay on task with for the time it takes to get the job done.

CAN YOU RELATE?

Although Vikram learns very well and has no real academic trouble, his parents are in a constant fight with him to actually complete his homework.

His parents decide to use their *physical proximity* as a nonverbal *prompt* to support Vikram's task completion. They have Vikram do his homework in a more 'public' space

4. TEACHING

at home — the dining room table — and they sit at the table with him while doing their own thing. They check in with him periodically, providing him with encouraging words and feedback, and rewarding him at the end for having completed his homework.

Not to worry, Vikram's parents will not have to sit with him through university for him to get his work done! They will 'fade' themselves out. Over time, a parent may sit with him at the beginning to make sure he gets started, then leave the table but stay pretty close so they can continue to provide encouragement and praise periodically. Eventually, Vikram will learn to sit down and get his homework done, providing himself with short breaks if it's a long project, and rewarding himself at the end with something he likes to do.

Modelling. Modelling, or showing by example, is another way of teaching your child how to start and finish a task without nagging, haranguing and begging. With modelling, you accompany your child in the initial steps of the task and show them the desired behaviour. This works well for the 'wall of awful' tasks — the ones that seem so big and awful your child cannot bear the thought of doing them. Cleaning up after playing, tidying bedrooms and kitchen clean-up are classic examples where modelling would be your strategy of choice.

So you might introduce the task, 'Time to clean up', with the added reassurance, 'Let's start it/do it together'. If it is a relatively straightforward task, pick up a few of the items yourself and then fade yourself out once your child is rockin' and rollin' with it. If it is a longer, more complex or more overwhelming task, you may want to stick around a little longer and do a 'talk aloud' of how you are approaching the task to break it down to make it more manageable: 'Time to clean up. Let's do it together. Wow, this looks like a big job. Let's start with the books. Let's get the books on the shelf.' When the books are away, you might pick a toy bin to fill with trains and tracks and then another with blocks … you get the idea … until the job is done.

What to do when TEACHing goes South

Let's face it. Teaching does not always go smoothly, to say the least. Lots of kicking and screaming at first, maybe some grumbling and belly-aching along the way. So what do you do when you are trying to teach and problem behaviours pop up?

Once a problem behaviour begins, teaching moments disappear. Do not attempt to continue active teaching.

Children cannot learn when they are upset. Parents cannot be good teachers when they are frustrated.

So, when teaching goes south, make a mental note about what might have gone wrong and plan to adjust your teaching strategies for the next time. This teaching opportunity is over, but do not give up!

Take a peek at our upcoming chapters on how to **Motivate** children, how to teach co-operation and how to teach other skills such as Emotion Regulation or completing the morning routine. If your child is struggling with one of these skills, we have great ideas for you coming up!

SECTION III

—

Motivate

5.

Understanding Reinforcement

We have all heard the term Positive Reinforcement and we know it is supposed to be a good thing for our kids. But what is it really? Is it praising your son for every good deed he does? Is it giving your daughter a treat every time she co-operates? Is it putting stickers on a chart so your child can see their good behaviour?

At its heart, Reinforcement is a simple concept: It increases the chances a behaviour will happen again.

> **SCIENCE SIDEBAR**
>
> In behavioural terminology, Positive Reinforcement is the presentation of a stimulus, after a particular behaviour occurs, that *increases the likelihood of that behaviour recurring.*

5. UNDERSTANDING REINFORCEMENT

Let's unpack that. It is one person giving 'something' such as an object, activity or praise, so the other person 'repeats' what they just did.

> Child Behaviour + Positive Reinforcement = Child More Likely to Engage in the Behaviour Again

Study after study has demonstrated that Positive Reinforcement is the most effective way to **Motivate**. It is the most effective way to promote long-term behaviour change. Keep in mind that *everybody*, including you, your spouse, your children, your parents and even your boss, responds to Positive Reinforcement. Check out some of these real-life scenarios of Positive Reinforcement in action:

CAN YOU RELATE?

You open the door for someone at the mall. They say thank you and you feel appreciated.

RESULT: You are more likely to open the door for someone the next time you are in a similar situation.

You check in on your neighbour's cats while they are on holiday. They are grateful for your help and bring you a bottle of wine.

RESULT: You are more likely to agree to look after the cats when they are away in the future.

> You put in extra effort on a job at work. Your boss sends out a company-wide memo to recognize your dedication.
>
> **RESULT:** You are more likely to put in extra effort on the next project.

For parents, using Reinforcement planfully and effectively **Motivates** children to behave in resilient, confident and likeable ways.

Key Elements of Reinforcement

Since Reinforcement is the most powerful **Motivate** strategy, it is very important for parents to have a clear understanding of the key elements of Reinforcement and how to use it effectively.

1. Positive Reinforcement must *increase* the behaviour you want to see.
2. Positive Reinforcement must be delivered *as soon as possible*.
3. Positive Reinforcement must be *contingent* upon your child's appropriate behaviour.

Going back to the questions in the first paragraph of this chapter, Positive Reinforcement is not simply praising your son for every good deed. Remember our definition. Positive Reinforcement *increases* the chances that behaviour will happen again. So it is only considered Positive Reinforcement if he starts doing more and more good deeds. In other words, giving him praise increases the behaviour you want to see.

5. UNDERSTANDING REINFORCEMENT

On the flip side, you could give your daughter a treat every time she does what was asked. But if she still only listens to your instructions once in a while, then that expensive candy you bought at the all-vegan, totally organic specialty store is not working as Positive Reinforcement.

And the sticker-chart example? A common myth is that stickers in and of themselves are a reward within a sticker chart. Unfortunately, for most kiddos, stickers are not going to be motivating or interesting enough to produce long-lasting behaviour change. This is especially true for difficult tasks or tasks that are just not interesting to the child.

SCIENCE SIDEBAR

'Increase' in behaviour can mean a few things:

> › You may want to see an increase in *frequency* (e.g., that your child listens to you more often).
>
> › You may want to see an increase in *quality* (e.g., your daughter clears all the dishes from the table, and stacks and rinses the dishes, rather than just bringing them to the counter and leaving them).
>
> › You may want to see an increase in *duration* of the behaviour (e.g., your son works on his homework for twenty minutes at a time rather than five minutes).

It is important that you and your child are clear on which kind of 'increase' you are working on/looking for.

Reinforcement in Action

Let's walk through a scenario of how Positive Reinforcement works to increase a wanted behaviour.

Tom's parents want him to wash the dishes after dinner. They make a deal with him that he can watch his favourite Netflix episode right after he has washed the dishes. This should reinforce his dishwashing. We would anticipate that he would be willing to wash the dishes again the next day.

> Tom does the dishes. Tom is allowed to watch Netflix.
>
> **RESULT:** Tom is more likely to wash the dishes next time.

Picture this scenario where Reinforcement gets delayed. With the same deal as above, Tom willingly washes the dishes. His mother is about to tell him to go watch his show but then his dad realizes there is a special news report at 8 p.m. Tom must wait for an hour before he is allowed to watch Netflix. He grumbles a bit about how that wasn't the plan and waits to watch Netflix. The next night, when asked to wash the dishes, he protests loudly and angrily about the injustice of it all. He is not motivated to wash the dishes the following evening.

> Tom does the dishes. Dad insists on watching the news after dinner. Tom watches Netflix after an hour delay.

5. UNDERSTANDING REINFORCEMENT

> **RESULT:** Tom does not wash the dishes the next night.

It is crucial for Reinforcement to be given *immediately*.

Now picture this scenario where parents inadvertently reinforce misbehaviour: Again, same deal as before, Tom willingly washes the dishes. His mum is about to tell him to go and watch his show but then his dad realizes there is a special news report at 8 p.m. Tom yells at Dad saying how unfair everything is, and stomps upstairs to his room. After seeing his big reaction, Tom's parents feel badly about the 'bait and switch' they pulled on their son. Dad offers to watch the news on his laptop instead and Tom is allowed to watch Netflix. Tom has learned that a tantrum will get him what he wants the next time he is told he must wait for something.

> Tom does the dishes with the promise of watching Netflix. Dad says he wants to watch the news. Tom yells and screams. Dad watches the news on his laptop instead and Tom watches Netflix.
>
> **RESULT:** Tom is more likely to tantrum again the next time he is asked to wait for Netflix. He is also less likely to do the dishes again.

It is crucial that the Reinforcement is given only following *appropriate* behaviours.

This is a very important point. As with the above example, Positive Reinforcement can sometimes accidentally be used to increase the behaviours we *don't* want to see.

Below are a few more real-life examples of how parents inadvertently use Reinforcement at the wrong time.

> **CAN YOU RELATE?**
>
> At the grocery store check-out aisle, Sam is screaming for a chocolate bar. His parents purchase the chocolate bar in order to stop the screaming.
>
> **RESULT:** Sam is more likely to scream the next time he wants something at the check-out.
>
> Billy has a playdate in half an hour. His mum asks him to do his homework before he goes. Billy screams and cries the whole time. Billy goes to his friend's house without his homework being done.
>
> **RESULT:** Billy is more likely to cry and scream to avoid doing his homework next time.
>
> Maya's dad asks her to go to bed. She asks for a snack, then water and then three extra stories. Her dad gives her the snacks, the water and extra stories.
>
> **RESULT:** Maya is more likely to try to delay bedtime next time.

5. UNDERSTANDING REINFORCEMENT

Stuart asks to play on the iPad. His mum hesitates because she is using it for work. Stuart throws a ball at her head. His mum scolds him and then gives him the iPad.

RESULT: Stuart is more likely to lash out at his mum next time she hesitates to give him what he has asked for.

Now let's apply this information about *when and how* to use reinforcement correctly within your own home.

PUTTING IT INTO PRACTICE

Before using reinforcement, it's helpful to consider, record notes and be aware of:

> - what behaviour you will reinforce
> - how well your child has to do it
> - if it is something they *can* do. If not, please refer to the chapters explaining how to **Teach** new skills.

After using reinforcement, reflect on its use, specifically if:

> - it was delivered immediately
> - the intended behaviour was reinforced

> problem behaviour did not happen immediately *before* you gave the reinforcer

> you provided praise to your child.

Consider how and when you will fade (give less) of the reinforcement over time.

Now we know more about Positive Reinforcement, it is important to consider how to identify effective reinforcers. Finding your child's 'currency' will need to be done in a thoughtful and planned way.

How to Find Reinforcers

Remember, everyone is motivated by Positive Reinforcement. The trick is to know what motivates a person in any given moment. What will make it worthwhile for your child to do something that is either not easy or not interesting to them? Getting a piece of that delicious vegan, organic candy may not be sufficiently motivating for a child who finds cleaning their bedroom to be very difficult and boring. Nor will it be motivating for a child who has their own stash of Halloween candy hidden away under their bed.

Parents have to **Prepare** before they can use reinforcers to **Motivate** their children. The first essential step will be to find that 'thing' that will motivate.

Reinforcing items can come from a range of categories. Often the best ones are those that naturally fit the situation. The common practice of allowing children dessert only after they have finished

5. UNDERSTANDING REINFORCEMENT

their meal is an example of a reinforcer that naturally follows the desired behaviour.

Not all situations allow for the use of naturally occurring reinforcers. Parents need to be flexible, change the reinforcers often and adapt them for the individual. There is no one thing that is universally reinforcing. There is no one thing that is reinforcing all the time. Some children like stickers, others crave praise and others require more intense activities such as tickles or water balloon fights. These can change from day to day. Stuffies may not be an effective reinforcer after Jill received three new ones for her birthday. Chocolate may not be an effective reinforcer the morning after Halloween. For parents, wine may not be an effective reinforcer during a hangover.

Most importantly, it is not a reinforcer because *you* like it, or because you think your child *should* like it. It is reinforcing because *your child* likes it and values it in that moment. You will know you have found a reinforcer when you see that it **Motivates** them to do whatever it is again in the future.

> ### SCIENCE SIDEBAR
>
> There are many different types of reinforcers. These may include:
>
> › tangible reinforcers, such as items, toys, foods, treats, things that feel or smell nice

> activities or privileges, such as swimming, board games, playing sports, watching TV

> social reinforcers, such as props/fist bumps, hugs, high-fives, kind words of appreciation

> or a combination of these, such as watching a movie and eating popcorn with friends.

Although the technical term for all these is 'reinforcer', you will see we use the term 'reward' to mean the same thing.

A few factors that may change how effective or **Motivating** your reinforcer is:

> Frequency: How often they get it.

> Intensity: How much of it they get (e.g., full attention of parent vs sharing it with a sibling; a bear hug vs a high five).

> Duration: How long they get it for (e.g., two episodes rather than one, an extra bed time story).

When choosing, or helping your child to choose, a reward, make sure it is something you can control, that you have time for, that you can afford and that you are willing to withhold if your child does not earn it. Reinforcement must be feasible if you want to have a sustainable and realistic teaching plan for your child.

5. UNDERSTANDING REINFORCEMENT

Think outside the box and get creative! You may have to experiment with a variety of items, activities and ways of giving attention before you find something that will actually work as a reward for your child. We have known kids who are willing to work on a new skill for a range of things … a quick game of hide and seek, the opportunity to tell a ridiculous joke, Pokémon cards, a five-minute dance party, being able to choose what is for dinner, and even cotton balls. It is perfectly acceptable to ask your older child what they would like to work for (within reason). It can be fun for parents to spend time with their child generating ideas for reinforcers.

> **PUTTING IT INTO PRACTICE**
>
> It's time to take out your Parenting Journal and find some effective reinforcers for your child in three steps.
>
> 1. *Create a list* of things you think your child would like as a reward. Watch and take note of the things they ask for or activities they enjoy. What are their current must-haves? Better yet, sit down and ask your child. Some categories of things they may enjoy may be Things to Do (e.g., stay up later, play video games), Things to Have (e.g., nail polish, new toys to play with the dog) or Things to Eat.
>
> 2. *Reality Check*. Consider the following points to help you decide if the items on your list will be an effective

reinforcer. And remember, just because it is not an effective reinforcer for this task and at this time, it might be effective later.

> My child currently does not have free access to it.
> I can afford it, both with time and/or money.
> The reward is worth the amount of 'work' my child is expected to do.
> I am willing to withhold it if my child does not earn it.

3. *Modify* your original list based on your reality check.

SCIENCE SIDEBAR

So far when we've been talking about reinforcement, we have been talking about it in the singular — a reinforcer, a reward — from one category, be it praise, positive attention, tangible, an activity, etc. In actuality any singular reinforcer is often a combination or synthesis of many aspects of the 'thing' that is enjoyable. This concept is called 'synthesized reinforcement'.

Take for example a video game. Your child may really like a particular game but they also get enjoyment from other aspects than just the game. They may like playing with others on-line, they may enjoy the break from being asked to do chores or homework, they may enjoy the snacks they eat while they are playing. So while 'the reinforcer' is the video game, in actual fact the act of playing the video game is a synthesis or combined effect of several enjoyable things. When choosing reinforcers, try to create ways to layer in things that will make it more enjoyable as a 'synthesized reinforcer'. It becomes much more powerful!

Reinforcing Versus Bribing

We can hear you thinking, aren't I just bribing my kid? What makes using Positive Reinforcement different from straight-up bribery? Good question! The short answer is *timing*. Remember that Positive Reinforcement is *contingent* on your child's appropriate behaviour occurring. Let's say it again, your child gets the reward *after* they have done what was expected. And it should only be given *before* any negative behaviour happens.

In contrast, a bribe is offered *after* your child has ignored your requests or engaged in other problematic behaviour. It is not pre-planned nor is it a part of a system of Positive Reinforcement. It is typically an effort on the part of the parent to get back on track when things have started to 'go south'. Bribery can quickly turn into begging your child to behave.

Let's remember our friend Tom and his dishwashing chores:

REINFORCEMENT

Mum asks Tom to wash the dishes. Tom does the dishes. Tom is allowed to watch Netflix.

RESULT: Tom washes the dishes next time.

Now picture this:

BRIBERY

Mum asks Tom to wash the dishes. Tom complains that he always has to wash the dishes and that it's his sister's turn. Dad strikes a deal and says he is allowed to watch Netflix and have popcorn if he washes the dishes this time.

RESULT: Tom is more likely to whine and complain next time he is asked to wash the dishes.

Tom did the job, right? Yes, but 'bribery' occurred while he was not co-operating to wash the dishes. He was given Netflix and popcorn *after* complaining. This could actually *increase* the likelihood of his complaining in the future! He may hold out on listening to his parents to wait for the better 'offer' of rewards in the future. If Tom associates positive outcomes with when he delays or avoids an expected activity, his parents may have started a cycle in which Tom will never co-operate until they negotiate and/or bribe him

5. UNDERSTANDING REINFORCEMENT

to do so. If you make the same mistake, what you have done by accident is reinforce a behaviour that YOU DO NOT WANT TO SEE.

> **CAN YOU RELATE?**
>
> There are some rare and specific situations in which it may be effective or even necessary to use bribery. These typically involve large public places, medical procedures or events where you really, really need your child to keep it together. In an airport security line. During a long wait at an amusement park. Getting a needle. At your cousin's black-tie wedding. In these situations, which typically do not happen all that often, it is okay to resort to whatever means necessary to get through with minimal outbursts and disruptive behaviour. Just be mindful of the fact that you are using bribery, *not* Positive Reinforcement, in these scenarios. Make a note of the skills your child may need to work on before you expose them to a similar situation again.

Reality Check: Can my child do this?

Reinforcement will only work if your child is capable of the skill you are targeting. This goes back to the ideas of **Teach**. In Chapter 3, 'Being a "Skills Detective"', we talked about selecting *achievable* goals for your child. Ensure your child is capable of the skill you are targeting and that the goal is achievable. No matter how large, shiny or fun your reinforcer/reward is, if your child is not actually capable of the skill at this moment, they will never receive the item.

You may be ready to offer a fantastic prize every time your daughter sits quietly through an entire meal. If she is not actually capable of sitting for more than three minutes at a time, she will never receive the prize. Ultimately, your system may feel more like punishment for her lack of ability rather than a positive system you had planned.

> **CAN YOU RELATE?**
>
> Would you take a million dollars if it was offered to you? What about if you were told that all you have to do is learn to speak fluent Latin within three days? For most of us, our excitement would quickly disappear, since we are not actually capable of learning a completely new language in three days. This would be a case of the reward being sufficiently enticing but the foundational skill being too far out of your wheelhouse to ever earn it.
>
> **RESULT:** You may react to this offer with indifference — 'oh well, I'm no worse off' — or with annoyance and anger — 'it was completely unfair to dangle the promise of loads of money for something you knew I wouldn't be able to do!'

5. UNDERSTANDING REINFORCEMENT

The 'DOs' of Using Reinforcement

So now you have an understanding of the science behind Reinforcement, here is a list of DOs to consider as you use Reinforcement to **Motivate** your child:

» DO catch your child being good and reward them quickly for it.

> Reinforcement works best when it is provided *immediately* following the behaviour you are targeting. When your child independently completes the three steps in the morning routine you have set as your goal, you must be ready to stop everything and follow through with your end of the bargain.

> Behavioural researchers have demonstrated for decades that immediately giving some kind of reward is a key factor in motivation.

> Due to time constraints, especially in the morning when families are all trying to get out the door, many of us try to delay the reinforcer until a time that is more convenient. Saying 'Good work this morning, Andy! We'll be sure to do the magic tricks tonight after dinner' probably will not work to **Motivate** him to get ready quickly tomorrow. And the chances of the reinforcer being forgotten all together, by either you or your child, are high.

» DO remember to use praise, even if you are also using an item or activity as a reinforcer.

- Remember you are teaching your child new skills and they need to know what and when they have done well.
- Even generic phrases such as 'good job', 'great work' or 'way to go' can be motivating and reinforcing if they are delivered in a genuine, sincere and enthusiastic way.
- On occasion, add some variety to your praise, like 'Hamza, you cleaned up your toys so quickly! Amazing!'
- Kids will eventually tune out praise if they sense it is not sincere or genuine.

» DO put as much or more *energy* and *intensity* into positive statements as you do when you are upset or disappointed.

- Some children find any kind of reaction or attention from parents rewarding.
- Kids who thrive on *intensity* may be more motivated by the intensity of your yelling, anger and frustration than your praise if your praise is quiet, generic and underwhelming for them.
- For example, if Susie gets a pat on the back every time she co-operates with a request from her mother, and she gets a two-minute lecture every time she does not co-operate, the longer and more intense lecture may actually end up being more reinforcing than a pat on the back. And what behaviour will be more likely to reoccur? You got it — the non-co-operation.

5. UNDERSTANDING REINFORCEMENT

» DO be aware that your child may satiate on, or 'get sick of', a particular item you are using as Reinforcement.

   › Even if your son loved that specialty candy initially, after he has been earning it for a couple of weeks, it may lose its power to motivate. He may revert back to his old ways, leading you to abandon the idea of Reinforcement altogether. In actuality, it is this particular Reinforcer that has lost its zing to increase the wanted behaviour.

   › Mix things up *before* your child has a chance to satiate on the reinforcer.

   › For young children, one excellent way to avoid satiation is to make a 'treasure chest' of rewards. This way, your child is allowed to pick something that is of particular interest to them in the moment. The best treasure chests we have seen are those that have lots of different items and lots of different activities written on slips of paper. Some fun items could be pieces of gum, trading cards, stickers or Lego pieces. Some fun activities might include a tickle fight, five minutes of shooting hoops with Dad, ten minutes to read books alone with Mum, a phone call to Grandma or extra TV time.

   › Keeping an eye on what your child consistently choses from the treasure box or list allows you to see what your child is really interested in. If he has never picked a balloon out of the box, then you know to find other items that will keep him motivated.

- For older children, spending some down time dreaming up a list of potential reinforcers (both items and activities) may be in and of itself a fun and rewarding activity.

» DO avoid offering rewards or reinforcement for every little thing your child does, especially for things they already know how to do.

- You could run into a situation whereby a child expects to be rewarded for easy and expected tasks.
- If you've ever heard your child say, 'I'll do it, but what is my reward?', then you may be guilty of continuing to reward a skill that is mastered.

» DO avoid negotiation!

- A huge advantage of having a predetermined system for using Positive Reinforcement is that you, your partner and your kids will already know the consequences for expected behaviour. This virtually eliminates the in-the-moment negotiations that are so often used by kids as stall tactics, threats and ultimatums to buy good behaviour.
- Thinking back to Chapter 4: 'Teaching', the 'First — Then' contingencies are already in place when you establish a plan for Positive Reinforcement so there is no need for further discussion.

5. UNDERSTANDING REINFORCEMENT

> If you find that your techniques, 'deals' or 'contracts' require refinement, that's okay. Do so at a later time. But don't negotiate about something that has already been set out.

» DO use the 80/20 Rule.

> Aim to provide four times the amount of Positive Reinforcement as you do corrective or negative feedback.

> This may sound easy but it is actually quite difficult to do. As humans, we tend to notice our own, our partners', our co-workers' and our children's mistakes, and are very quick to point them out, as compared to how often we notice their positive behaviours.

> We know that children who receive praise and acknowledgement for their good choices are more likely to repeat those choices over time. But, if the Reinforcement is buried under a mountain of corrections, blame and punishments, then you may have undermined your own Reinforcement efforts!

> This is especially important for those children who, because of developmental lags, behavioural issues or difficulties regulating their emotions, receive a lot of corrective feedback over the course of the day.

> **CAN YOU RELATE?**
>
> A simple mantra to keep in mind is, 'Praise the best and ignore the rest'. It is a bit like what our grandparents used to say to us: 'If you don't have anything nice to say, then don't say anything at all.' Give it a try — you'll find that it works! And the whole family will feel happier when the focus is on the positive and not on the negative.

» DO remember that you can use Reinforcement to decrease problem behaviour as well.

> › Wait, what? Didn't we just say that Reinforcement *increases* the behaviour that we want to see? Yes, thanks for remembering that.☺ But, the sophisticated behaviourist knows that parents can reinforce the *absence of problem behaviour*. So, even if your child did not engage in any really great behaviours during your trip to the grocery store, you can still provide a Reinforcer for the lack of tantrum behaviours, if that is a goal you have set.
>
> › When reinforcing the *absence of problem behaviour*, reward often and immediately (e.g., when there are no tantrums in the grocery store or no hitting on the car ride to school).
>
> › And if you remember our chapters on 'Being a "Skills Detective"' and 'Teaching', you can also teach *alternatives* to the problem behaviour. Rather than having Tim run up and down the aisles at the grocery store, you can teach him

5. UNDERSTANDING REINFORCEMENT

to get items and load them in the cart as an alternative. Voilà, you now have a behaviour you can reinforce.

» DO give an increased amount of Reinforcement for times when your child really hits it out of the park.

> For example, if you have set a goal of having your son make his bed every morning, and one day he not only makes his bed but he tidies his room and makes his sister's bed too, go ahead and give him double the Reinforcer he was entitled to.

> This concept is called 'Differential Reinforcement' and it means parents can change the quality (in terms of amount, intensity, or duration) of Reinforcement based on the quality of the response from their children.

> Use Differential Reinforcement sparingly to avoid your child feeling they deserve 'extra' every single time they do something really well, or something very difficult.

» DO fade your Reinforcement over time.

> Do it gradually and in a planned way. We don't want to go from providing our children with Reinforcement every time they do something well to giving them nothing. So plan ahead for how to make your decisions.

> For example, let's say you start by giving your son, Amil, a Pokémon card every time he makes his bed. You might decide that after one week, if he has earned his card on six of the seven days, you will change how often he earns his

Reinforcement to once about every two days. So now, Amil has to do the task twice before he earns his reward. Then after another week, you may move to providing a card after every three days, and so on.

> Another method for fading Reinforcement is to add in another skill. So if Amil makes his bed on six out of seven days, the following week you may want to ask him to put his clothes in the hamper as well. He still earns a Pokémon card, but he has to do two things instead of one.

> Once your child is consistently making his bed, you could keep him guessing a little bit about when he will get a Pokémon card for making his bed by switching to 'Intermittent Reinforcement'. This means that once you know he knows how to make his bed, you give a Pokémon every once in a while, to let him know you still appreciate his bed making and to maintain his motivation to keep making it.

> You will know if you are decreasing the Reinforcement too quickly if your child stops engaging in the desired behaviour. If that happens, you can move back to the previous level (e.g., every time they make their bed), without overt frustration or dismay, and try to reduce the reinforcement again in the future.

5. UNDERSTANDING REINFORCEMENT

SCIENCE SIDEBAR

Science tells us that Intermittent Reinforcement is extremely effective in maintaining and continuing behaviours. Once a behaviour has been learned, providing reinforcement *unpredictably* keeps people guessing as to when they are getting the reward. As a result, motivation stays high.

Think of a slot machine where you may receive a small reward on the seventh pull, or the 109th pull, or you may hit the jackpot on the 37th pull. This Intermittent Reinforcement keeps people gambling. Similarly, we want to encourage our children to 'gamble' that their good behaviour will reap them big rewards.

The dark side of this coin is that as parents we often teach our kids to gamble on the effectiveness of their bad behaviour. Think of when you gave in to your child after the tenth time they whined for something or after the twenty-minute tantrum when you've said 'no'. You have effectively taught them to hold out for the 'jackpot' and to 'keep feeding the machine' until you give in.

Trouble-Shooting

To end this chapter, we would like to trouble-shoot some common problems parents face when using Reinforcement to **Motivate** their children.

1. 'We have tried everything but there is nothing that is an effective Reinforcer for my child.'

    > We hear this a lot. We know it can be very difficult to find an item or activity that is reinforcing for some children. However, with creativity and perseverance, we have found there are Reinforcers for all behaviours, as long as the behaviour is something your child is capable of. So do not give up!

    > For some children, when they are allowed free access to a variety of items and activities, it makes it very difficult to build motivation. If your child has unlimited screen time, receives new toys frequently or can access the snack cupboard on their own, you could try restricting some of these privileges temporarily in order to build their desire for these things.

    > Try the 'Treasure Chest' that was described earlier in the chapter. The issue could be that your child has sufficient interest in many things, but the variety is what really gets them going.

    > Talk to your child and ask them what they would like to earn. They might surprise you with their answers! Keep an

5. UNDERSTANDING REINFORCEMENT

open mind about what they ask for but remind them there are time and financial limits.

› Consider ways you can incorporate or combine other reinforcers (take a peek again at our Science sidebar on synthesized reinforcement on p. 96).

› And before throwing out your reward system, have another look at whether or not your child can actually do the task you are asking of them. Check that the effort to complete the task is not overwhelming for them.

2. 'We have been offering favourite rewards to our son, but he is still not earning them as often as we would like. What are we doing wrong?'

› It could be that the task is too hard for him. Can he actually do what you are asking him to do? In situations in which a task is too difficult, even the most wonderful rewards will not be effective because he has to work too hard. He can do it, it just takes sooooo muuuuuch effffort. Behaviourists refer to this concept as 'response effort'. The payout for your child has to be worth it for the amount of work that they have to do.

› One approach to overcome this situation is to break the task into smaller parts and reward him for successful completion of each small part. When the child is successful, you can gradually increase the expectation. For example, if you want your son to clean up the kitchen after dinner, you could start by having him load the dishwasher with dirty dishes and rewarding him for that. As he learns this skill, you can then increase the job to having him load the dishwasher and wipe the counters. And so on.

› It could be that the child does not have the skill at all, and so you will need to teach him (just like we talked about in Chapter 3: 'Being a "Skills Detective"' and Chapter 4: 'Teaching'). In the kitchen clean-up example, this means you may have to start by loading the dishwasher with your son, teaching him exactly where everything goes and how you want the dishes put in. It may take a while before he has learned how to do the task independently, so you provide Reinforcement along the way so he stays motivated.

3. 'I don't understand it, but my daughter seems to actually dislike it when I praise her for her good behaviour. What do I do?'

› Again, this is a common scenario in our private practices. Some children appear to react negatively in response to praise. Remember, there is nothing inherently Reinforcing about praise — we can only be sure that it is a Reinforcer if we see an increase in the behaviour we are trying to teach.

› Some kids prefer more subtle reactions from parents, such as a thumbs-up, a wink or a pat on the back. If these things work to increase the desired behaviour, then go for it!

› Be careful that you do not accidentally ask her to do more work or give her a correction immediately after your praise. Some examples might be, 'You did a great job with

5. UNDERSTANDING REINFORCEMENT

the dishwasher! Now go scrub the pots', 'Thanks for tidying your room; can you also come and unpack the groceries for me?', 'Awesome homework today! Next time you should double-check your spelling.'

4. 'Our Reinforcement plan worked well in the beginning, but lately we have had to give our daughter more rewards than we did before in order to get her to do her chores.'

   › This is a tricky situation, to be sure. The goal is to fade rewards over time, not increase them. If you find that your child is having less and less success with the behaviour you are teaching them, take a step back and review your plan. It may be that the behaviour is actually too difficult for them. It may be that they are satiating on the Reinforcer. It may be that you have been delaying the delivery of the Reinforcer.

   › We strongly recommend you avoid increasing the Reinforcer once a plan has been started. If a child learns they can earn more by doing less (or by complaining about what they have to do), then they may use the system to their advantage.

   › It is okay for your daughter to not earn the reward. Even though you know she can do the task, she can choose not to perform it. Missing out on the reinforcer is a learning opportunity and she may discover her chores are worth it when she goes without the reward for a day or two.

5. 'Jean-Philippe is learning to get dressed by himself as a result of our Reinforcement plan, but he almost always has a tantrum first.'

   › In this example, parents have accidentally taught Jean-Philippe a sequence of behaviours. While they appropriately rewarded him for getting dressed they also rewarded his tantrum.

   › Be sure to have a clear idea of the behaviour you want to see. Also be clear about the behaviours you do not want to see. For example, you can specify that the goal is for Jean-Philippe to get dressed by himself, *without complaint*, every morning.

6. 'I don't want to reward my kid for this. I want them to want to do it.'

   › They don't want to do it. If they did, they would already be doing it.

7. 'If I give them so many rewards, won't I kill their internal motivation to learn?'

   › Internal motivation occurs when we act without any external rewards. We simply enjoy an activity and the feelings of pride or satisfaction that come with completing a task well.

   › Note that when behaviours are already internally rewarding there is no benefit from adding external motivation. In fact,

5. UNDERSTANDING REINFORCEMENT

if you give Reinforcement for a behaviour your child already enjoys, they may lose motivation over time. For example, if your child enjoys colouring, you do not need to provide any Reinforcement. On the other hand, your daughter may enjoy more drawing time or new drawing materials as rewards for learning to do the tough stuff.

› Teaching skills your child may otherwise never choose to do by using reinforcement allows them to discover enjoyable activities and to learn skills. This is a bigger gift than waiting for 'internal motivation' that may or may not evolve on its own.

› If your child is not motivated, you have to build the motivation externally. The best way to build internal motivation is to start with external rewards or Reinforcers. Even a desire for praise, your approval or just to please you would all be considered forms of external motivation.

› Begin with rewards and reinforcers as described in this chapter and, over time, decrease their use in a planned way. This will increase your child's feelings of competence, internal motivation and satisfaction over time.

› Just like there are no universally reinforcing items, there is nothing that would or should be internally motivating for everyone. Not everyone is naturally motivated by task completion, a clean home or academic success.

8. 'I know Positive Reinforcement is supposed to be effective, but it just seems so much easier to use punishment instead.'

   > In some ways it does seem easier to use punishment. We know that it takes some careful thinking to set up, use and keep a plan for Positive Reinforcement going. However, the research and our clinical experience is very clear: Positive Reinforcement is the single-most effective **Motivate** strategy available to us as parents. We cannot emphasize that enough. So if you really want to see long-term behaviour change, you must include Reinforcement in your parenting repertoire.

   > In the short-term, punishment can work quickly to reduce unwanted behaviours. But it does little to teach a child what they need to know. And it comes with several unpleasant side effects such as instilling fear of punishment or of the punisher (parents), having new unwanted and unexpected behaviours pop up, and needing more and more intense punishers over time.

   > In fact, when teaching many skills, there is actually no need for punishment at all. Think of all the many things your child has already learned (walking, biking, reading, dressing, etc.). We would wager a bet that you did not use any punishment strategies when teaching these skills. You are very likely using lots of Positive Reinforcement strategies already.

   > That said, there are some situations when use of punishment strategies could be considered. We strongly encourage

5. UNDERSTANDING REINFORCEMENT

parents to have a solid system for Positive Reinforcement in place before adding mild and planned punishment. In other words, be sure you have a good grasp of the content in this chapter before moving on to Chapter 6: 'Understanding Punishment'.

9. 'When can I stop using Reinforcement?'

   › The short answer is Never. Remember we are all motivated by Reinforcement. When is the last time you went to work for free?
   › What we are motivated to do, and what motivates us, may change over time, but Reinforcement is still important.
   › Once a skill is mastered and the Reinforcement has been gradually removed, new goals may be selected.
   › As parents, our job is to teach our children to be independent for a variety of tasks so there is always room to be working on the next thing. As they get older, the tasks will become bigger and your expectations will increase, but some level of Reinforcement will be helpful at every stage.

6.

Understanding Punishment

So here it is. The chapter you've all been waiting for: punishment! Notice we have left the discussion about punishment until the very end of this section. That was intentional. We strongly believe that punishment is the *least important* aspect of the **Prepare. Teach. Motivate.** strategies. You may disagree. We hope to convince you of this fact by the end of this chapter.

Remember from the chapter you just finished, reinforcement *increases* the chances of a behaviour happening again in the future. In contrast, punishment *decreases* the chances of a behaviour happening again in the future.

6. UNDERSTANDING PUNISHMENT

> **SCIENCE SIDEBAR**
>
> To recap, Positive Reinforcement is the presentation of a stimulus, after a particular behaviour occurs, that *increases the likelihood of that behaviour recurring*.
>
> Punishment is the presentation or removal of a stimulus, after a particular behaviour occurs, that *decreases the likelihood of that behaviour recurring*.
>
> Child Behaviour + Punishment = Child Less Likely to Engage in that Behaviour Again

Remember, if you punish unwanted behaviour without teaching and reinforcing appropriate behaviour, the punishment will not be effective in the long term. Kids need to learn what to do, not just what *not* to do. Moreover, if they do not actually have the skill you want to see, punishing them will not be effective. Can you imagine punishing your toddler for having toileting accidents when they do not know how to use the potty or wipe themselves properly yet? Punishing kids for skills they do not have could be quite detrimental to your relationship and their self-esteem in the long term.

When we work with parents, some of their first questions inevitably relate to how best to punish problem behaviour to make sure it never, ever happens again. Parents often feel the need to use punishment to show their children the behaviour was wrong. We also often feel the need to show others (other parents, teachers, in-laws) that we know our child's behaviour was wrong.

CAN YOU RELATE?

We hear lots and lots of questions and comments about the necessity of punishment:

> 'Yes, yes, we now know that we need to reinforce the good behaviour, but don't we have to do something in response to the problem behaviour too?'
> 'Won't our children just learn they can get away with being bad?'
> 'By *not* punishing bad behaviour, won't I encourage it?'
> 'My kids will think I'm a pushover and they just keep taking advantage of me.'
> 'I need my kid to learn they can't act like that in the "real world".'
> 'In the real world there are consequences for your behaviour.'

The list goes on. Let's just say that none of these concerns is unfounded and none of the questions wrong. We are simply suggesting a different approach to teaching and motivating your child to act in resilient, confident and likeable ways.

6. UNDERSTANDING PUNISHMENT

Here's the thing: we do not actually have to do anything in response to problem behaviour. Mind blown.

We know this is hard for parents to wrap their heads around, but we will say it again. Consequences for misbehaviour are not actually necessary ... most of the time.

When parents use **Prepare. Teach. Motivate.** (with Positive Reinforcement), we believe there will be little need for this chapter ... most of the time.

In fact, in the six chapters that follow this one, the chapters in which we discuss effective **Prepare. Teach. Motivate.** strategies to deal with the trickiest parenting situations, punishment is mentioned only once. Just. Once.

In many situations, parents will be able to decrease unwanted behaviour by 'ignoring it' or 'waiting it out' (but not giving in). By giving little attention, discussion, access to preferred items or emotional reaction when our children misbehave, we are showing them their misbehaviour has no effect. Once they see their misbehaviour does nothing for them, it will decrease over time.

Remember what we said about praising the best and ignoring the rest?

Believe us (and the science!) that praise and other forms of Positive Reinforcement for our children's good behaviours will be sufficient to increase the intensity, frequency and duration of their good behaviour over time ... in most cases.

But please also remember that all kids are going to demonstrate problem behaviour from time to time. That is okay. Not only is it okay, it is expected. It does not necessarily mean you need to start punishing your child for every misbehaviour.

Children are learning what is acceptable and what is not. During this process, they will inevitably make mistakes and do things that are not-so-nice and not-so-acceptable. Our role as parents is not to *eliminate* any and all problem behaviour. Our role is to *decrease* the frequency, duration and intensity of misbehaviour over time. We do not necessarily need punishment to do that.

Getting Rid of Unwanted Behaviour Without Punishment

By now, we hope you have a good understanding of **Prepare. Teach. Motivate.** We also hope you have developed a plan to **Prepare. Teach. Motivate.** (with Positive Reinforcement) your child. If you happened to jump to the 'Understanding Punishment' chapter first, please take the time to read the previous chapters. We promise it will be worth your while.☺

However, even with the other strategies in place, your child may still be misbehaving and you would like them to stop. Before discussing creative punishments, let's take a minute to learn about a non-punishing, but highly effective tool to motivate your child. It is called 'extinction'.

> **SCIENCE SIDEBAR**
>
> Behaviour scientists define extinction as the process of *withholding* a *reinforcing consequence.*

6. UNDERSTANDING PUNISHMENT

In essence, extinction is an *unlearning* process. Somewhere along the way, an accidental connection has been made between a misbehaviour and getting something good or at least something that is wanted in that moment (the misbehaviour has been reinforced). Extinction is the process of breaking that link. To do this, you really have to figure out what your child is after in the moment and not 'give in' to it. Recall our 'Skills Detective' chapter that provides some guidelines on how to quickly figure out what your child is after in the moment.

CAN YOU RELATE?

Four-year-old Sanjay tantrums in the grocery store check-out line when he is told he is not allowed to buy any gum. His father, in desperate need to get out of the store before things escalate, gives in and buys a pack of gum.

RESULT: Sanjay's tantrum has been reinforced with the gum. He will likely tantrum when in similar situations in the future.

When twelve-year-old Anna is asked to feed the pets, she slams the door to her bedroom and cranks her music. Her mother, wanting to keep the peace, feeds the pets herself and leaves Anna alone.

RESULT: Anna's slamming of the door has been reinforced by avoiding a demand. She might act that way the next time she is asked to help out.

> Five-year-old Mia spits out her food every time her mother holds her baby brother. Her mother promptly puts the baby down in order to reprimand Mia and then spoonfeeds her while talking about why spitting is not acceptable.
>
> **RESULT:** Mia has been reinforced by the attention from her mother. She will probably continue spitting out her food whenever her mother is occupied with the baby.

In each of the above examples, the parent has accidentally taught the behaviour they do not want to see. They have reinforced and made the connection between the child's misbehaviour (Sanjay's tantrum, Anna's door slamming and Mia's food spitting) by 'giving in' to what their child wanted in each of those situations (gum, avoidance, attention).

For all these situations, extinction could be an effective motivation strategy for unlearning. By not 'giving in' the children will, over time, stop engaging in the undesired behaviours because those behaviours stopped getting them what they wanted.

Keep reading and you will see that we don't need to punish the behaviour out of our children; we just need to stop reinforcing it.

> Child (mis)Behaviour + No Reinforcement (don't give in) = Child Less Likely to Do the Behaviour Again as a way to get what they want

Re-visiting the above examples, using extinction might look like this:

6. UNDERSTANDING PUNISHMENT

Sanjay tantrums in the grocery store check-out line when he is told he is not allowed to buy any gum. His father acknowledges Sanjay's disappointment, purchases the groceries and not the gum, and calmly carries Sanjay out of the store.

RESULT: Sanjay's dad has used extinction because he has not reinforced Sanjay's tantrum by buying him gum. Sanjay will be less likely to tantrum when in similar situations in the future.

When Anna is asked to feed the pets, she slams the door to her bedroom and cranks her music. Her mother follows through with her request for Anna to help out by bringing the pets and their food up to Anna's room.

RESULT: Anna's mum has used extinction by not reinforcing the door slamming. Anna will be less likely to try this when asked to help with the pets the next time.

Mia spits out her food every time her mother holds her baby brother. Her mother ignores this and continues to provide attention to the baby.

RESULT: Mia's mother has used extinction by not attending to Mia immediately after she spat out the food. Over time, Mia will learn that spitting out her food whenever her mother is occupied with the baby does not get her the attention she wants.

Before we go on, we need to let you in on an important, counter-intuitive and potentially distressing fact. When using extinction, the undesired behaviour may actually *increase* in intensity, duration and/or frequency for a brief period. This happens because your child is testing to see if you will give in if they amp up a little ... or a lot. But if you are able to hold your ground, and you stand firm, the undesired behaviour will stop. This is a well-researched behavioural phenomenon known as an 'extinction burst'. It can and should be expected whenever extinction is used.

CAN YOU RELATE?

Consider the following example of an extinction burst. You are expecting to enjoy a cold soda after finishing the gardening chores — a positive reinforcer, if you will. You try to twist off the cap but you are unable to get it open. Do you just give up and walk away? Not likely! You would work harder to open that bottle. You may try to use a belt buckle. You may try to wedge it off with your teeth. You may try to slam the top of the bottle against the corner of the brick wall while swearing at the blasted thing. All these increasingly aggressive attempts to open the bottle constitute an extinction burst. However, after a while, you would probably resign yourself to the fact you cannot access this particular bottle of soda, give up for good and look for something else to satisfy your thirst.

6. UNDERSTANDING PUNISHMENT

In a parenting situation, we must be very, very careful to avoid reinforcing a child when they are in the midst of an extinction burst. Because next time, the child might *start* at the elevated level of problem behaviour and escalate even further. They have learned to make darn sure they get what they want the first time. Imagine if the cap had flown off that bottle after swearing at it and slamming it against the brick wall? Slamming and swearing may become your go-to the next time you had a bottle that needed opening, because sometimes it works.

> Sanjay tantrums in the grocery store check-out line when he is told he is not allowed to buy any gum. At first, his father stands his ground and still does not buy the gum. Sanjay ups the ante by increasing his volume and kicking his father's legs. His father, embarrassed at the check-out, relents and buys him the gum.
>
> **RESULT:** Sanjay's father has accidentally reinforced Sanjay's *more* intense tantrum by giving him the gum. Unfortunately, Sanjay will probably start at this *increased level* of tantrum when in similar situations in the future.

Extinction is an effective tool for children to 'unlearn' that their misbehaviour will get them what they want. But it does not **Teach** them what to do instead to get them what they want. This brings us back to the point we have been making throughout this book — **Prepare. Teach. Motivate.** are highly interconnected.

Let's go back to our friend Mia and her food spitting.

> Mia spits out her food every time her mother holds her baby brother. Her mother ignores the spitting and continues to provide attention to the baby. At another time, when she is not holding the baby, Mia's mother teaches Mia how to ask for attention appropriately. It might sound something like this: 'Mia, you can say, "Excuse me, Mummy" when you want me, ok?' Then her mum playfully asks Mia to practise saying that phrase and Mia's mum immediately turns to her daughter, tickles her and they both have a good laugh.
>
> **RESULT:** Mia's spitting has been put on extinction *and* she has learned a better way to get her mother's attention. Having learned how to get her mother's attention, Mia is more likely to use the phrase 'Excuse me, Mummy' rather than spitting out her food the next time her mother is holding the baby. Her mother then can briefly pause attending to the baby and ask Mia what she needs/wants.

The takeaway message from the above example is this: While using extinction to break the cycle of reinforcing unwanted behaviour, find ways to **Teach** your child the skills that they are missing. Mia's

6. UNDERSTANDING PUNISHMENT

mother realized she needed to teach her daughter a better way to get attention.

Things to Consider Before Using Punishment

So what do you do when you cannot figure out what connection you have accidentally reinforced? What do you do when you've tried to use extinction to get rid of an undesired behaviour but it has not worked?

Let's exhaust our possibilities. Let's review how to really make sure we are using Reinforcement and Extinction effectively. Before considering punishment and before reading on, ask yourself the following series of questions:

» Was I offering a reinforcer/reward my child actually wanted at that moment?
» Were my expectations truly reasonable?
» Was the balance of how hard it would be to stop doing the misbehaviour (or do something else) and the value of the reward in sync? (i.e., was it worth it?)
» Did I really use extinction right to the bitter end? We know that sometimes life takes over and the situation needs to move on. It can be very difficult to truly 'wait it out' or to 'ignore' the misbehaviour all the time.

If you can honestly, in your heart of hearts, answer 'yes' to the above questions, then punishment may be an appropriate next step. When combined with the other **Prepare. Teach. Motivate.** with Positive Reinforcement, punishment can be a useful parenting tool.

Still, we encourage parents to limit the circumstances under which they would use punishment at all. Punishment should be reserved for extreme circumstances. Completely over the line behaviour. To our minds this would be limited to acts of aggression or destruction of property.

A Word on Physical and Emotional Punishment: DON'T

When people hear the word 'punishment' they might think of physical or corporal punishment, including smacking, belting, spanking, biting back or washing out mouths. Corporal punishment is harmful and even illegal in many places. There are safer, more humane and, most importantly, more effective behaviour change strategies that do not involve these outdated approaches.

To be clear, punishment *should never involve physical intervention.*

The research has shown it is not effective in creating long-term, lasting, positive changes in anyone's behaviour. It simply does not work. Add to that the fact that repetitive use of physical punishments can result in serious, long-term emotional problems in children.

In the same vein, humiliating, debasing or publicly embarrassing our children are not acceptable forms of punishment. All punishments must be mild, brief, humane and dignified.

Do not use physical or emotional punishment. End of story.

6. UNDERSTANDING PUNISHMENT

> **CAN YOU RELATE?**
>
> If you find yourself using physical, corporal or emotional punishment, in any form, please consider reaching out to family services in your community to work on developing healthier and more effective parenting strategies.

Options for Punishment

In our professional opinions, there are really only three forms of humane and effective punishment that are available to parents:

1. Time-Out
2. Removal of privileges
3. Natural consequences

Time-Out

For young children, 'Time-Out from Positive Reinforcement' or more commonly known as simply 'Time-Out', is a widely used strategy. The goal is to remove all fun activities for a *short* period of time. This is not a time to distract the child with something else or to force them to think about the terrible things they have done. It is not even a time for them to 'calm down'. It is simply a time for them to sit apart from the action. They can sit alone on the stairs, in a corner or on a chair removed from others.

General consensus is that a Time-Out should last for as many minutes as the age of the child (e.g., a four-year-old child should have a four-minute Time-Out). Use a timer you and your child can both see in order to be precise and consistent. But remember, Time-Out can be effective with the younger crowd, usually children under the age of seven.

> Child Behaviour + Time-Out from Reinforcement =
> Child Less Likely to Engage in that Behaviour Again

Entire books have been written on the principle of Time-Outs. It sounds like a simple strategy, but there are some common mistakes that can make it ineffective at best, and actually reinforce the problem behaviour at worst:

1. Engaging with the child during their Time-Out, even if it seems like a 'negative' interaction. Remember that for some children any kind of interaction may be engaging and reinforcing, even if it is in the form of a lecture, scolding or reprimanding.
2. Trying to teach during the Time-Out. This is not a time to work on breathing exercises or other forms of self-regulation. It is simply a time away from the fun.
3. Responding to tantrums and/or engaging in negotiation. The Time-Out starts when the child is staying in the designated place (chair, step, etc.), regardless of whether they are quiet. If they leave the space, pause the timer and gently return them without discussion.

6. UNDERSTANDING PUNISHMENT

4. Lecturing the child after the Time-Out. Once the Time-Out is over, they can return to their previous activities. There is no need for lengthy discussions or forced apologies. They have served their time and they can now return to the fun.

> **CAN YOU RELATE?**
>
> Avril hits her little sister. The *planned* consequence is for her to have a three-minute Time-Out. Her mother takes her to her room. While Avril kicks and screams all the way, her mother calmly explains that she can leave her room once she has been quiet for three minutes. Mum proceeds to hold the door closed while Avril kicks at it, tries to get out, screams and generally escalates the intensity of her emotional reaction. It takes over 30 minutes for Avril to calm down, by which time both she and her mother are exhausted and can barely remember what led to the Time-Out in the first place. Note that this example assumes Avril's mother was actually able to wait outside her door for 30 minutes. Who was supervising the little sister during this time? Was her mother compelled to let her out early because Avril was breaking things in her room? Or maybe her mum gave up because she did not think it was worth the effort.

Time-Out does not work for all children. Many will not 'accept' their Time-Out. This happens when the child refuses to stay in the

Time-Out spot, when they engage in ongoing problem behaviours, such as spitting, destroying or throwing anything in reach, or when it escalates their emotional reaction to a point that they cannot learn from the punishment.

If this is your situation, you may be parenting a child who will not accept Time-Out. That's okay. It's not for everyone or every child. In that case, it will be best to cut your losses and read on for other punishment strategies.

Removal of Privileges

Removing a preferred item or activity for a short period of time can also be a powerful punishment. These days, the removal or reduction of screen-time privileges can be used very effectively as motivation. Of course there are other options, but in our experience, most kids place a very high value on screen-time, and because it is non-essential (it's true — screens are not actually required for our survival!), it can be taken away without concern.

> Child Behaviour + Loss of a Privilege = Child Less Likely to Engage in that Behaviour Again

What to remove?

Take a moment to consider what is a 'privilege' for your child. If you are co-parenting, be sure to have this conversation with your parenting partner. Some things are obvious privileges ... screen-time, dessert, a new toy, a trip to the movies ... but some are in a grey area. Is it a privilege to host a sleepover? To go to a basketball practice?

6. UNDERSTANDING PUNISHMENT

To attend a school trip? These things are certainly not *essential*, but they do add plenty to the social and emotional wellbeing of our children.

Another thing to keep in mind when thinking of privileges to remove is how realistic or willing you are as a parent to actually remove it. Threatening to not celebrate a birthday, to cancel a family trip or to tell Santa not to bring any presents at Christmas may feel like powerful motivators, but are you really willing to follow through with any of them? Are you really going to cancel the party? Are you really going to lose the deposit on the hotel? Are you really going to return all the gifts under the tree? These removals are simply unrealistic and unlikely to happen as they impact too many other people in the family.

In general, we do not suggest removing social events, exercise/sports, birthday parties or fun school activities as punishment.

For punishment, parents should never withhold something that is necessary for their child's health, safety or physical wellbeing (such as meals, exercise, clothing, shelter, etc.). No matter how significant the misbehaviour, we must always meet our children's basic needs and provide a loving and safe environment.

How long to remove a privilege?

We advise thinking carefully about how long you are going to remove a preferred item or activity. Keeping in mind that the goal of using punishment is to reduce the future occurrences of misbehaviour, a short loss of privileges (e.g., one hour or one day) is just as effective as a longer punishment (e.g., two weeks or two months). There are a few reasons why this is the case:

1. If you remove a privilege for a long period of time, you may lose your leverage for future misbehaviours. For example, if your son has lost Xbox access for two weeks because he swore at his little sister, what happens when he engages in the same misbehaviour a day later? Adding punishment to another punishment (i.e., now he has lost Xbox access for three weeks) is not a sustainable option: parents will usually find they give in before the punishment period ends.

2. Removal of the privilege for long stretches will mean parents need to find activities to fill that time. Not doing so may result in *more* misbehaviour, because for this long stretch of time your child literally has 'nothing (of value) to lose'. Moreover, parents may feel as though they are being punished by having to entertain their children ... while the children are actually enjoying the increased attention and engagement. Often parents will end the punishment early because it is taking up too much of their time.

CAN YOU RELATE?

If you find you are regularly increasing the length of your punishment (i.e., it started as one week but then went to two weeks, and then three...), you may want to re-examine your strategies and try to use shorter periods when removing privileges.

6. UNDERSTANDING PUNISHMENT

3. Another reason to avoid lengthy punishments is that the immediacy factor is reduced. Do you remember that Reinforcement is most effective when it occurs *immediately* after the behaviour you are trying to increase? The same is very true for punishment. If a child receives a week-long punishment (such as lost time to play with a preferred toy) the teaching moment is lost long before the punishment runs out. The child may not even remember why they were being punished in the first place.

4. A final point on the duration of punishments: if we return to the idea that we want to emphasize a child's good behaviour and draw limited attention to their misbehaviour, it is virtually impossible to do this in the midst of a lengthy punishment. How can you tip the balance to focus on the positive behaviours when your child is enduring a lengthy removal of a preferred activity? Nothing you can say or celebrate will compare to them being disallowed something they enjoy.

The take-home message is this: keep your punishments mild, realistic and brief.

Natural Consequences

The final punishment strategy is to capitalize on the natural consequence of the misbehaviour.

> **CAN YOU RELATE?**
>
> Marko did not complete the bedtime routine quickly.

RESULT: Marko did not have time to watch an episode of his favourite TV show before bed.

During a tantrum, Jayda threw and broke a favourite toy.

RESULT: She could not play with the toy again until her parents had time to fix or replace it.

Matthew did not finish his homework before bed.

RESULT: Matthew had to wake up early the next morning in order to complete it before the due date.

Natural consequences are similar to taking away a privilege, but they unfold organically in the situation. In general, we do not plan for them, but we can take advantage of them as motivators when the situations arise.

SCIENCE SIDEBAR

You may have heard the term 'negative reinforcement' and you may think this is another term for punishment. We want to clear the air on this one. *Negative reinforcement is not punishment.* Let's repeat that: Negative reinforcement is not punishment.

6. UNDERSTANDING PUNISHMENT

In geeky science-speak, negative reinforcement is the removal of an aversive stimulus (an object or activity) after a particular behaviour occurs that *increases the likelihood of that behaviour recurring.* It is the removal of something someone does not like in order to encourage them to do what you want them to do.

To illustrate, imagine the last time you uttered these words: 'I would stop nagging you if you would just clean your room.' The undesired stimulus (nagging) stops when the desired behaviour happens (room cleaning).

Child Behaviour + Remove Something Aversive = Child More Likely to Engage in Behaviour Again

In reality, parents do not usually use negative reinforcement on purpose. However, we thought it important to include a short sidebar on the topic because we are very tired of hearing the term misused. ☺

The 'DOs' of Using Punishment

Please keep in mind that using punishment is a last resort. It is used only after you have **Prepared** your child to do the right thing, **Taught** your child to do the right thing and **Motivated** your child to do the right thing with Positive Reinforcement.

Now that you have an understanding of the science of punishment, here is a list of DOs to consider as you think of ways to **Motivate** your child:

- » DO remember that all punishments should be *mild* and *brief.*
    - › Short time-outs or a brief loss of privileges are just as effective and easier to implement than lengthy punishments. They also allow for better management of future good and bad behaviour.

- » DO ensure that punishment is predictable.
    - › Just as when you develop a Reinforcement plan, prepare ahead of time for what behaviours will result in punishment and what the punishment will be.
    - › Discuss your expectations for your child's behaviour ahead of time so everyone knows what the punishment will be for inappropriate behaviour.
    - › This eliminates the need for creativity and negotiations, and ensures you and your parenting partner will be consistent. As always, good preparation will increase consistency and effectiveness of any parenting strategy.

- » DO avoid using punishment when you are angry.
    - › Being rational and calm models good behaviour and will allow you to enforce a punishment that is fair and effective.

6. UNDERSTANDING PUNISHMENT

- › The implementation of increasingly aversive punishments tends to be about the parent's emotional state and not about the child's misbehaviour. Again, having a plan ahead of time will reduce the need to punish 'on the fly'.
- › It is always okay to step away for a few minutes, wait until your own mood has settled and then come back to calmly impose the punishment.
- › Because parents are human beings, there are times when we will get angry or upset in front of our kids. An occasional flare-up is not necessarily a terrible thing. When you are calm and reasonable 95 per cent of the time, it can actually make the 5 per cent of the time when you lose your cool a valuable teaching moment. Showing moderate anger on rare occasions can make your kids take notice. As in, 'Wow. I must have really crossed the line.' It also provides an opportunity for you to model apologizing for your behaviour after the fact.
- › A final point about anger: If you are finding that you are becoming more and more easily angered by your child's misbehaviour and that your reactions are becoming more extreme, *seek professional help*.

» DO avoid threats of punishment when you have no intention of following through.

- › 'Listen to me or we will go home right now' will only work if you actually mean it.

> You can provide one warning about the upcoming punishment for your child's behaviour and then you *must* use punishment if the behaviour re-occurs. This will teach your child that you say what you mean and you mean what you say. Children learn very quickly what their parents will and will not do. One of the biggest mistakes parents make is to lose credibility by threatening to do things they never actually do.

> If you know you will be unable to follow-through with a punishment for misbehaviour it is better not to threaten it in the first place. Some factors just get in the way of you being able to follow through: you are in a public setting, you are not feeling well, your attention is focused on something else, etc. In these cases, it will be much better to not react to the child's behaviour than to threaten something you cannot do.

» DO keep in mind that the effective ratio of Reinforcement to punishment is at least 4:1.

> If you find you are using more punishment than reward, you may need to re-think your approach and/or expectations.

> It is very difficult to maintain a high ratio of Reinforcement when your child is in Time-Out multiple times per day or if they lose a privilege more often than they have access to it. So it makes sense to use punishment only for a child's serious mistakes.

6. UNDERSTANDING PUNISHMENT

- » DO avoid implementing a new punishment when there is one already in place.

  - › This situation can be avoided by providing short punishments for misbehaviour.
  - › If your child engages in problem behaviour while they are still serving their punishment for a previous one, it is best not to change anything and let the current punishment run its course.
  - › If you find you are implementing back-to-back or overlapping punishments for problem behaviour, you probably need to adjust your strategy and/or lower your expectations for achievable behavioural goals.

- » DO be aware of entering into the vicious cycle of punishment.

  - › When we implement a punishment for an unwanted behaviour and it does not work (meaning the misbehaviour occurs again), our natural instinct is to then increase the amount of punishment we use. And then when that does not work, we increase it again … and again … and again. At some point our child has to clue in and realize that we don't want to see this nasty behaviour, right?
  - › If this is happening to you and your child, the problem behaviour is re-occurring not because they secretly love the punishments you are giving nor because they love manipulating the system you have developed. In all likelihood, they are engaging in the problem behaviour

because they do not have the skills to do anything different in that situation.

> › Escalating cycles of punishment are a sure sign that the Fundamentals of **Prepare. Teach. Motivate.** with Positive Reinforcement have fallen by the wayside.

» DO resist the urge to allow your child to earn back a privilege once it has been lost.

> › For example, if a child loses screen time, but then engages in really positive and kind behaviours, we often want to reward the good behaviour by removing or decreasing the punishment.
>
> › Our advice is to avoid this. If you follow the other punishment principles we have described here, there will not be many times when a child can earn something back early because their loss of the privilege was only for a brief time anyway.
>
> › Additionally, the option of earning back privileges opens the door to negotiation and inconsistency between parents. When parents want to decrease or end a punishment before the agreed upon timeframe, it is often the result of implementing an overly harsh consequence in the first place or of being tired with having to maintain the plan.

6. UNDERSTANDING PUNISHMENT

> **PUTTING IT INTO PRACTICE**

There are an incredible number of considerations regarding punishment. Some common questions are included below. You will notice that we want you to strongly consider using **Teach** strategies, particularly being a 'Skills Detective', and the **Motivate** strategy of Reinforcement, before deciding to add in punishment.

› Why is the behaviour happening?
› What else has been attempted other than punishment?
› What am I teaching instead? How am I reinforcing the alternative?
› Were my expectations truly reasonable?
› Was I offering a reinforcer/reward my child actually wanted in that moment? Was the reward worth the effort?
› Is it *reasonable* to punish this behaviour?

It is worth repeating, in our clinical practices, it is *highly unusual* for us to require or tell parents to use punishment procedures. We, too, have to persevere as Skills Detectives so we can determine appropriate alternative skills to teach. Use of punishment cannot be substituted for appropriate detective work and teaching skills.

Once you have thoroughly considered the above, if challenges persist and you decide to use punishment, ensure it is *reasonable* to punish the behaviour. This bears repeating. Ensure that punishment is a reasonable response to your child's behaviour. Be sure you are clear and specific about the following:

> *What* behaviour is being punished.
> *How* it will be punished (e.g., Time-Out, removal of privilege, natural consequences).
> *When* it will be used.
> It is *mild and brief.*
> It is *humane and dignifying.*
> It is feasible.

Trouble-Shooting

To end this chapter, we would like to review some common problems that parents face when implementing punishment as a means to **Motivate** their children.

1. 'I understand the concept of Reinforcement, but for my child, punishment is the only thing that works.'

    > This is a frequent comment from parents and we know that it can seem like punishment is the only thing that changes a child's behaviour. In fact, punishment can be an

6. UNDERSTANDING PUNISHMENT

   effective short-term solution when you want a behaviour to stop immediately.

   › However, the research on child development and behaviour is clear: punishment is not a good long-term solution. We *guarantee* that you will continue to see problem behaviour unless you add in the other parenting fundamentals: **Prepare. Teach. Motivate.** (with Reinforcement).

   › Remember, any problem behaviour is an indication of one or more skill deficits. Teaching your child how to behave better is the ultimate goal. Simply trying to 'stamp out' problems via punishment will keep the problem behaviour, or variations of the behaviour, around for a lot longer and keep you in a revolving game of 'whack-a-mole'.

2. 'I have tried to ignore my daughter's bad behaviour, but she just ramps it up until it is impossible to ignore her any longer.'

   › This happens all the time and is an example of the extinction burst we referred to earlier in the chapter. When an expected reinforcer (such as that item they are seeking) is not provided, children will increase the intensity or duration of their behaviour in order to try to get what they want.

   › In a situation like this, parents have two choices. They can work extra hard at withholding the item, knowing if they 'give in' to the more intense level of the behaviour, the child may well just start off at that level next time.

> The other option is to work extra hard at avoiding these situations by emphasizing the **Prepare. Teach. Motivate.** (with Reinforcement) aspects of their parenting plan.

> Avoid providing Reinforcement for the increased level of problem behaviour. This will definitely make the situation worse the next time.

> Be honest with yourself. If you know you will not be able to ignore a certain behaviour or if the behaviour will escalate to a level that cannot be ignored, then ignoring cannot be an effective part of your plan. And that is okay. As reviewed in this chapter and the one on 'Understanding Reinforcement', there are other ways to **Motivate** children that may work better for your family. No single solution will work for every family or in every parenting situation, so allow yourself the time to learn what fits for you.

3. 'I punish my son all the time, but it never seems to really work to change his behaviour. Now we are at the point where he has almost no privileges or fun left in his life. What do I do?'

> It sounds as though this parent has inadvertently fallen into a cycle of increasing punishment.

> As parents, it is normal and natural to feel the need to increase the level of punishment when it does not seem to work the first time (e.g., taking the electronics away for five days instead of one day). And then we increase it again (taking the electronics away for two weeks) and again (now

6. UNDERSTANDING PUNISHMENT

electronics are gone for a month) in an effort to show our kids that we mean business.

> An increasing cycle of punishment is a sure sign that **Prepare. Teach. Motivate.** with Reinforcement are missing. If you find yourself in this position, it is time to conduct a complete reset. We recommend you focus all your efforts on **Prepare. Teach. Motivate.** with Reinforcement and remove punishment completely, at least for a while.

> After a period of escalating punishment, it will be especially important to put in extra effort with regard to Quality Time. You will find that increasing your focus on happy, positive interactions will go a long way toward counteracting any possible damage that has happened because of too much punishment.

4. 'My kids seem to accept their punishments without even caring. Sometimes they even laugh at me. I need some ideas about how to punish them hard enough to make it work.'

> Hopefully, at this point in the chapter, you know that there is no such thing as punishing a child 'hard enough'. Short and mild punishments are the only effective options.

> If you find punishment is not an effective strategy for your child, so be it! Remember, punishment is not necessary to change a child's behaviour.

> Emphasize **Prepare. Teach. Motivate.** while being a 'Skills Detective' and using Reinforcement to prove you can change your child's behaviour without punishment!

5. 'My daughter loves to negotiate and we always get into lengthy discussions about what is a fair punishment. I want to include her in the decision-making but it feels like it is getting extreme.'

   > We support the idea of including kids in the decision-making regarding a plan to increase their good behaviour and/or decrease their not-so-good behaviour. Collaboration and negotiation are good skills to develop.

   > However, there is a time and a place for negotiation and collaboration, and the moment in which a parent issues a punishment is definitely not it.

   > Make plans with your child during calm and happy times, and listen to all their ideas. Encourage problem-solving, creativity, skill-building and compromise. Once the plan is in place, write it down and post it where everyone can see it. There is no need for further negotiation.

   > If your child attempts to negotiate once a punishment has been levied, calmly refer to the plan. We do not want children to learn that negotiation (or begging, pleading, crying or threatening revenge) will get them out of the punishment.

6. 'My partner and I have developed a parenting plan that includes lots of Reinforcement and a bit of punishment. However, I seem to be the only one who implements the punishment piece and I worry my kids are starting to see me as the bad guy.'

   > This is an unpleasant situation, to be sure, and not at all uncommon.

6. UNDERSTANDING PUNISHMENT

› If this is happening in your family, it is time for a calm discussion with your partner about parenting roles and responsibilities. Although things can never be perfectly balanced, the ideal situation is when *both* parents are using Reinforcement and punishment according to the agreed-upon plan.

› If such a discussion does not work to change things, then you have the option of eliminating punishment from the plan completely. Keep in mind that behaviour change can and does occur without punishment. It may be more important to have the children view you equally (with no 'bad guy') than to have one parent implementing all the punishment alone.

SECTION IV

—

Prepare. Teach. Motivate. in Action

7.

Just Do It!
Teaching co-operation

CAN YOU RELATE?

'Scotty, It's time for dinner! Please put away your toys, wash your hands and come to the table. Oh, and would you mind feeding the cat on your way?' Five minutes later, there has been no movement.

Now again, with a bit more volume, Mum says, 'Did you hear me? I need you to put away your toys, feed the cat, wash your hands and come to the table. Now! I mean it!' Five more minutes pass, and nothing. Mum is starting to fume. Dinner is getting cold and the kids need to get to karate on time.

7. JUST DO IT

> She storms up the stairs, sees Scotty playing quietly in his room and decides to move in with a threat: 'Young man, if you don't get yourself to the table in one minute, there will be no TV after karate tonight. Do you understand me?' Scotty groans, throws his toys down, stomps to the table, slouches in his chair and says, 'I'm here. Happy now?'
>
> **RESULT**: Mum is definitely not feeling happy. But at least Scotty finally complied with her requests, or at least one of them, right?

So … what is co-operation anyway?

Basically, co-operation is when children do what they are asked to do, when they are 'good listeners', and when they follow our instructions. People often use the word co-operation when referring to children's *compliance*, and you will find that we use the terms interchangeably throughout this chapter.

Co-operation sounds like a simple thing, but it is not. Not only is it a rather complicated skill, it is a *crucial* one. If your child is not co-operative, it will be very difficult, if not impossible, to teach other skills. In our clinical practices, co-operation is the *single-most important skill* we teach because it is the foundation for everything else.

Let us repeat ourselves: CO-OPERATION IS THE SINGLE-MOST IMPORTANT SKILL to raising resilient, confident and likeable kids.

Like riding a bike, co-operation is a skill and, like all skills, it has to be learned. We know some kids are naturals when it comes to following instructions from their parents and others are not. If your child is one of those who only co-operates following endless negotiations or threats of increasingly harsh punishments, then roll up your sleeves! This chapter is for you.

My Kids Are Co-operative. Or are they?

Before we get into the nitty-gritty of what co-operation IS, let's spend a moment thinking about what it is NOT. There are four basic forms of non-co-operation:

1. *Passive non-co-operation or ignoring.* Your child simply does not do what you have asked them to do. They have tuned you out. Or even more blood boilingly insulting is when they agree to do it, yet they just don't. They are not angry or hostile, but they simply have no intention of doing what you have asked.
2. *Simple refusal.* Your child acknowledges your request but indicates by their words or gestures that they do not intend to comply. Still aggravating but less insulting, we think, than the first. With simple refusal, there is usually no anger associated unless you persist or try to force the issue.
3. *Direct defiance.* Here come the fighting words. Your child is openly peeved and hostile that you have dared to interrupt them to ask them to do ANYTHING. There could be anger, overt resistance, threats to freak out or actual freaking out (throwing things, hitting someone, hitting themselves, damaging something, etc.).

7. JUST DO IT

4. *Negotiation*. Don't be fooled. Your expert debater and mini-United Nations negotiator is attempting to bargain, compromise or make promises if you let them off the hook this 'one' time. They will suggest alternative solutions to doing what you have asked or will try to 'strike a sweet deal' to see how badly you want this done and what they can get out of it. They are not co-operating.

> **CAN YOU RELATE?**
>
> Kids may have a preferred MO, their 'go to' way of not listening to you, and they may have perfected it. Or they may be systematic about it and escalate through ignoring, negotiating and simply refusing, and then end with active hostility and defiance. Or they may put their 'non-compliance playlist' on shuffle just to keep it interesting. In any event, the end result is that they have not done what you have asked.

There is also 'fake co-operation'. We often hear parents say their children do co-operate. Indeed, their kids do eventually listen, perhaps only partially ... but only after endless nagging, negotiating, promises of big payoffs or actual begging. 'Fake co-operators' might also be complaining, stomping, slamming, slouching, swearing as they do what you've asked to show you how angry they are about having to comply. We are here to tell you that is NOT cooperation. Sure, maybe the job got done, but your child was not co-operative.

At the beginning of the chapter, Scotty only 'co-operated' after much waiting, repeated requests and yelling from his mother. Ultimately, he followed only part of the request. To be clear, this was not co-operation.

Managing non-co-operation, in any of its forms, is exhausting for all parties and will not work long-term. Sure, your negotiator might be on their way to an Ivy League Law School, or your passive non-complier may be perfecting their meditation techniques by tuning you out, but you will see that their tactics become increasingly intense, their demands become more and more outrageous, and their non-compliance becomes more entrenched.

By letting our kids off the hook when they negotiate, ignore, defy and refuse our requests, we are inadvertently teaching them to be less co-operative. Think back to how reinforcement works: by *regularly* giving in, we are increasing the likelihood they will be non-co-operative in the future.

Understanding Co-operation

There are three key characteristics of true co-operation when your child (or anyone else for that matter) is asked to do something. Assuming the request is something they can actually do on their own, then co-operation occurs when:

1. they do it when they are asked the FIRST time (ok, maybe the second time/with one reminder)
2. they do it WITHOUT complaint
3. they do it within a REASONABLE amount of time.

7. JUST DO IT

Sound blissful? It is. Sound impossible? It isn't. But it may take a little effort on the part of parents to **Teach**.

Before we get into the how-tos of creating this parenting paradise of children happily helping out, a few notes on how to **Prepare** by managing expectations.

How much co-operation do we really want from children? How much should we expect? The first answer that pops into our heads is that children should listen. Just listen. Period. On first blush this sounds about right but is it actually reasonable?

For an answer about reasonable expectations, let's look to the science. Clinical experience and the literature in developmental psychology tell us that when using the above definition of co-operation, typically developing children comply about 70 per cent of the time.

That's right, 70 per cent of the time.

This means it is natural and normal for kids to *not* co-operate 30 per cent of the time. As much as we may want our kids to co-operate with each and every request, we are not trying to raise robots. In fact, as they grow older, we want our kids to be creative, independent and critical thinkers who don't accept all things as they are.

SCIENCE SIDEBAR

Behaviour analysts always start by collecting baseline data. Baseline information tells you where your child is starting from, before you implement your **Prepare. Teach. Motivate.**

strategies. This is good science protocol and it also makes for good parenting practices.

Let's begin with some baseline data to see how often your child co-operates.

Although it may seem that your child NEVER listens, it may be worthwhile to record some facts.

Pull out your Parenting Journal and take some notes:

1. Count how many requests you make. Be sure to include all of them, even the very small and easy ones, in your overall count (this will be important information for later).

2. Count how many times your child did what you asked — the first time, without complaint and within a reasonable amount of time.

3. Divide the number of times your child co-operated by the number of requests you made.

Again, keep some perspective on how much co-operation is reasonable. If your number is 70 per cent or over, recognize that your child is complying as much as would be expected, pat yourself on the back for your exceptional parenting skills and feel free to skip the rest of this chapter. If your number is less than 70 per cent, or if you want to fine-tune your child's co-operation, read on!

Co-operation is a Skill

When co-operation does not come easily for a child, you have to **Teach** it, just like you would teach any other skill your child is lacking. As a comparison, let's think about teaching a child how to ride a bike.

Some kids are naturals — they get on a bike, they figure it out, and they ride. But most kids require preparation and a lot of teaching and a lot of practice before they have mastered the skill of bike-riding (and even still, they may wipe out on occasion).

When we teach children how to ride their bike, we **Prepare** them for success by making it easier for them — we may use a balance bike or training wheels to start. We **Teach** them with specific instructions on what to do with their eyes, their hands, their feet. We model and practise how to steer and how to brake. Then, when we feel that they are ready, we **Motivate** them as they practise putting it all together. We may run alongside them, motivating, encouraging and cheering them on, as they pedal with greater skill and confidence.

And when they fall off (which they all do at some point), we are caring and supportive. We may need to replace some of the supports (such as training wheels) we had thought they were ready to do without, and practise more. We don't get angry with our kids when they fall — we realize they are doing the best they can while they learn this new biking skill. When they are successful, we celebrate enthusiastically.

The same should go for teaching co-operation.

Teaching Co-operation

Let's see how to apply our three parenting fundamentals to teach the crucial skill of co-operation. If you have not already done so, we strongly encourage you to read (or re-read if it has been a while) the chapters describing **Prepare. Teach. Motivate.** In this section we will highlight the aspects that are particularly important for teaching co-operation. A good understanding of these Fundamentals will make it easier to understand and implement the following suggestions.

When teaching co-operation, remember it actually involves *two* people: 'the Asker' (the parent) and 'the Askee' (the child). Each person has different roles and responsibilities.

The parent's job	The child's job
1. Say what you mean — give a clear instruction.	1. Attend to the instruction (notice, acknowledge or orient toward the Asker).
2. Mean what you say — follow through with your expectation that it gets done.	2. Follow the instruction (the first time they are asked, without complaint and within a reasonable amount of time).
3. Make it happen again — reward co-operation.	

7. JUST DO IT

Let's Start with the Child's Job

Notice that the first job of the child is to attend, and respond in some way, to the instruction. This is a very important point so let's spend a moment trying to understand how and why kids put 'Mummy on Mute' or develop 'Daddy Deafness'.

In our busy and demanding day-to-day lives, sometimes it seems like we only talk to our kids to nag, correct, instruct or interrupt them from something they like. How many requests or negative comments a day do we give our children compared to positive comments or interactions? Interactions and comments that children have with their parents on any given day are, more often than not, negative, instructive or corrective. It's no wonder they *learn* to tune us out! Even as behavioural experts, we make mistakes too. Our own kids have cringed, rolled their eyes when we call their names, and even given us nicknames like the 'Ruiner of Fun'.

Children quickly learn it is not really worth it to pay attention when you call their name. So, before tackling teaching or re-teaching your children to co-operate with your requests, they may need to *unlearn* a negative association with hearing your voice. We suggest that you **Prepare**, by taking the time to start associating your voice, or your calling their name, with something good happening.

> **SCIENCE SIDEBAR**
>
> We first mentioned the concept of 'Pairing' in our 'Setting the Stage' chapter. Remember that you want to associate and *pair* yourselves with positives. It's kind of Pavlovian

> but basically, yes, you want your kids to 'salivate' with good expectations when you call their name rather than 'seethe' with anger. Small and frequent positives across the day will *pair* yourself with those positives and increase the likelihood your child will co-operate.

Doing this is kind of simple and it can be quite fun. When things at home are calm, quiet and going well, take time to do some pairing. Instead of backing away slowly, afraid to 'poke the bear' that may be residing inside your lovely child, we suggest you call their name and then give them something they like (such as a kiss, a wink, a tickle, a tic tac, positive comments, praise or demonstrating interest in what they are doing). They may giggle, smile or even brush you away, but you are on your way to 'pairing' yourself with good things again. After a few days of doing this, you can move to the next step. When you call their name, if they don't respond with some kind of remotely polite response like, 'ya?', 'yes, Dad', or 'okay', quietly ask them to do so. Literally ask them to practise it. And when they do? You guessed it ... reinforce it. It's a behaviour you want to see happen more often.

> **SCIENCE SIDEBAR**
>
> There is research demonstrating that when children regularly acknowledge when their name is called they are much more likely to co-operate when they are asked to do things!

Once they get used to you calling them for good reasons again, you will no longer only be the 'Ruiner of Fun' (although let's face it, sometimes it is in the job description of being the parent). Now you are prepared to **Teach** them to co-operate with what you ask them to do ... the first time, without complaint and within a reasonable amount of time.

Now You Have Their Attention

Let's go back to the tasks of the Asker, the parent. If you are doing your job right, your child will learn to do their job right.

The first task of the parent is to ask. Although, technically, to deliver an effective instruction you are actually *telling* more than you are asking. As soon as you start with 'do you want to ...', 'who wants to ...', 'could you ...', 'would you ...,' you are creating an opportunity for an honest 'no' response. You gave a choice and they responded. As parents, when you actually need or want them to do something, please don't ask them *if* they want to do it. Simply state your request.

Here are the basic 'DOs' for delivering effective instructions when you are teaching the skill of co-operation. As always, you will notice that being proactive and prepared *before* you even give an instruction is essential.

PREPARE. Before asking:

» DO pick your moments and your battles carefully.

> › This is probably the single-most important proactive strategy when it comes to teaching co-operation.

> Now go back to the data you collected. How many requests are you actually making in a day? Probably a lot. Probably more than you mean to. Probably lots that you did not even realize you were making.

» DO be selective.

> Give demands only when you are quite confident your child will co-operate. Believe it or not, one of the key strategies for improving co-operation is giving *fewer* instructions. Nobody likes a drill sergeant.

> The timing of your instructions is *very* important.

> Make sure you are increasing the likelihood of 'yes' by not interrupting a favourite activity. Asking Jamal to clean up his room in the last three minutes of the FIFA Finals won't be successful (unless he hates soccer).

> Give instructions only when you are prepared to follow through and maintain the expectation it gets done. We often feel we have to be consistent with our expectations. There may be many reasons you are not able to follow through.

CAN YOU RELATE?

'Say what you mean' and 'Mean what you say'. If you know you don't have it in you to follow through or maintain the expectation because you are in the middle of the grocery store, are ill or if you have a strong suspicion time will run

7. JUST DO IT

out before your child is finished, just do it for them without asking. It ISN'T non-co-operation if you DON'T ask them to do something in the first place.

- » DO make sure you have your child's attention
    - › Get down on their level, be near them, be in front of them, make physical contact and/or wait for a 'yes, Mum' response.
    - › If they do not stop what they are doing, at least for a second, to acknowledge you, model it out for them and practise it. For example, you could say, 'When I call your name, please say, "Yes, Mum" or "Okay, Dad".'

- » DO ensure they can do it on their own.
    - › If they cannot do the job without help, do not even ask them to do it. Just help them. 'I am going to help you brush your teeth.'
    - › Put this on your list of skills you may wish to teach your child (see the chapter on 'Teaching').

- » DO create opportunities for them to co-operate and say 'yes' to you.
    - › Make easy requests during low-key times. This is so you can increase your opportunities to reward them, and then they will be more likely to co-operate.

> These small requests might include, 'Drink some juice', 'Turn on the TV', 'Please go skateboarding', 'Take this piece of Lego', 'Give your puppy a tummy rub'.

> Remember: What's easy for one child, might not be easy for another, and what's easy one day, might not be so easy the next.

SCIENCE SIDEBAR

Getting them on a roll of listening to you is called 'behavioural momentum'.

» DO give your child a heads-up when you must interrupt a preferred activity.

> E.g., 'Mary, in five minutes I want you to pack up the Lego.' Then repeat your request when the time has run out.

> A timer can be useful in these scenarios to make sure everyone keeps on track.

TEACH. How to ask:

» DO tell; do not ask.

> Although being told, the request can be given in a warm and respectful manner. 'Please take the dog out for a walk.'

- It is okay to confirm your child's understanding by asking at the end of the request if they 'got it', but avoid asking for their agreement by asking 'okay?' 'When this show is done, turn off the TV, got it?' is better than 'When this show is done, turn off the TV, okay?'

» DO use as few words as possible.

- As parents, we can get sucked into the 'talking trap'. We often feel we need to justify our requests, rules or boundaries, and we may just give TMI (too much information). Kids may love this, because the longer we talk, the longer they have postponed co-operating. On the other hand, all our talking usually confuses matters. Keep your instructions as short as possible.
- 'Andy, please pick up your toys' will be more effective than, 'Andy, remember that we have tutoring tonight, so I really need you to pick up your toys now. We have to pick up Mary on the way and we don't want to be late like we were last time.'
- Remember that the negotiator is technically being unco-operative to a request. If your child needs a reason why you are asking/telling them to do something, a *brief* explanation is enough. You can provide a longer explanation after they have done what you have asked/told them to do.

» DO remember the KISS principle — Keep it Simple, Stupid.

- Give your child one thing to do at a time.

» DO repeat your request only once.

> As parents we often continue to repeat our requests ad nauseum with increased volume and frustration — 'Put your dishes away.' 'I said to put your dishes away.' 'Listen to me now — I need you put your dishes away!'
> If your child does not start to co-operate with your request within 30 seconds, ensure you have their attention and repeat the request one time.
> Mean what you say. When we keep repeating our instruction (they have to listen eventually, right?) and the child is *not* following our request, we might actually be teaching them *not* to co-operate with our instructions.

» DO offer choices when they are available and appropriate.

> Respect your child's decision. Some children will learn co-operation more easily if they feel they have some control over the situation.
> For example, you may tell your child they can either pick up their toys or set the table before dinner.
> Keep in mind the choices are up to you, not your child, and that choices are only on offer *before* any non-co-operation occurs.

» DO use an *If — Then* sentence to clearly explain the natural consequences of their actions or inactions.

7. JUST DO IT

> This makes the connection between their co-operation and something *good* happening very clear.

> *If* you finish lunch by 12:30 — *Then* you can have more time to play.

> *If* we get all our groceries quickly — *Then* we can decorate that cake together.

> *If* you finish your homework before the party — *Then* you can stay for an extra hour.

» DO use your manners when you give instructions.

> Remember, the goal is to raise *likeable* kids. It is good modelling and it also increases the likelihood your child will co-operate with what you want. As parents, say 'please' and 'thank you'!

MOTIVATE. After asking:

» DO remember the definition of a 'reinforcer'.

> Something can only be called a reinforcer if it actually increases the likelihood of the behaviour occurring again.

> If your child is willing to bypass the reward, then three things might be happening:

- you are not dealing in the right currency for the situation
- you are not offering enough currency for the situation, and/or
- the instruction is too hard.

» DO reinforce the behaviours you want to see more often.

> If your child is compliant, even with a fairly easy task, notice and celebrate it! Your praise, attention or small tangible rewards are key to ensuring your child will be co-operative in the future.

» DO keep your promise when your child completes the 'First' part of a 'First — Then' instruction.

> They've kept their end of the bargain so it is essential you keep yours. We want our kids to know 'we mean what we say'.

> DO limit your talking while your child is doing what was asked.

> This includes correcting, reprimanding, entering into negotiations, cajoling, bribing, as well as falling for diversionary tactics such as off-topic conversations and questions.

» DO follow through with your requests. And this is what we mean by follow through.

> To be clear, follow through is not meant to be heavy-handed, and most of the time it does not involve hands on at all. When the 'First' part of your instruction does not happen in the specified way, even after you've repeated the instruction one time, DO help them to get it done in a warm and supportive fashion. Let them know they can have another chance at the 'Then' tomorrow, later or next time.

7. JUST DO IT

- › Even if you know what you are asking them to do is in their 'wheel-house', remember they are learning to do it the first time asked, without complaint and in a reasonable amount of time.
- › If they allow your help as you follow through with your request, they can earn part of the reward you promised. Keep in mind the principle of differential reinforcement (i.e., vary the amount, duration or intensity of the reinforcement so children get more when they do a better job).
- › Try not to huff, scold or otherwise express your disappointment. If your child does not have the *skill* of co-operation, then it is not fair to be upset with them for not demonstrating it.
- › Avoid giving extra attention, discussion and/or emotion when following through (i.e., doing it for or with them). If they get 'more of you' when they are not listening than when they are listening, you may very well be inadvertently reinforcing or rewarding their non-compliance.

» DO NOT reward/reinforce your child if they act defiantly, become aggressive, take excessively long to make a choice, attempt to negotiate or do not allow you to help them follow through.

- › They were not co-operating.
- › You want to communicate to your child, through *your behaviour*, that good things happen for them when they do good things.

> Keep calm, use a warm and respectful tone and act like their unco-operative behaviour is not bothering you (even if it really, really is!).
> Complete the task yourself, without discussion, in a down-to-business fashion.
> Try again at another time, ensuring to **Prepare** them for success.

Keep in mind that no child is co-operative 100 per cent of the time. If a particular interaction did not go as well as you had hoped, do not take it personally. Take a moment to reflect on what you could do next time to increase the likelihood of your child's success. Several tricky situations and suggested solutions are below.

Troubleshooting

Here are some ideas to address common problems when teaching co-operation.

1. 'My child co-operates with my requests, but only after I repeat them multiple times and with a raised voice.'

    > This is all the more reason to say your request calmly and to repeat it only once. Remember, repeating the instruction more than once while amping up your volume only promotes 'Daddy Deafness' and encourages your child to ignore you. You are accidentally teaching your child to listen only after multiple requests or only when your voice is raised.

> After making a request calmly, and repeating it only one time, be sure to reinforce their co-operation. If they don't start complying within 30 seconds, support them by following through and help them get the task done.

2. 'I offer lots of choices, but my child says she does not want to do any of them' or 'My child takes a very long time to decide which task he will complete.'

    > **Prepare** by being cautious about the number of choices you provide. If a child cannot make a decision about which to choose, you may be offering too many options. If they refuse to make a choice or they take a long time, this would be considered non-compliance. You will have to make the choice for them and help them complete the task.

3. 'When I give multiple instructions, only one or two of them get done.'

    > Remember KISS.
    > Divide your instructions into multiple steps. Only give one or two instructions at a time. Rather than saying, 'pause your game, go and wash your hands, empty the dishwasher and then come for dinner', try 1) 'pause your game' (praise); 2) 'wash your hands then empty the dishwasher' (praise/reward); 3) 'come for dinner' (praise).

4. 'My child is very curious and he needs lots of explanations before he will comply. Won't I harm his cognitive development by talking less?'

    > In short, no. While we absolutely encourage fulfilling children's curiosity, there is a time and place. It is important for your child to learn to co-operate with your requests without delay. When giving the instruction, a *brief* explanation can be provided, such as 'clean up your room, your friends are coming', rather than a lengthy explanation of the social importance of a clean room, the possibility of their friends judging them or the ability to find their favourite activities to play with their friends. If they are genuinely interested, offer to explain all this after the job is done.

5. 'My child will not do anything without the promise of a reward — I want her to learn to comply just because I said so!'

    > We agree! The ultimate goal is for your child to co-operate 'just because'. Remember what was discussed in the 'Understanding Reinforcement' chapter. When teaching a new or challenging skill, like co-operation, it is important to reward your child to motivate them to co-operate again in future.

    > Just as importantly, as your child becomes more co-operative, gradually decrease the intensity, frequency and/or duration of their rewards for the easy stuff. Eventually, rewards will not be needed every time.

7. JUST DO IT

- You may need to keep giving praise and rewards for co-operating with much harder tasks (like turning off their tablet). Reinforcers are proportionate to the difficulty of the task.

6. 'My child has excellent co-operation. I just have to make everything into a game.'

    - It is fantastic your child can co-operate well, but they do need to learn to co-operate outside of a game, a race or competition. In the real world, not everyone is willing to make it a game to gain co-operation. The game and party can happen *after* they have co-operated with your request!
    - To break this cycle, begin by presenting easier instructions without a game and rewarding your child's co-operation. As they become more co-operative about easy tasks, gradually increase the difficulty of what you ask. But keep those easier tasks in there in order to maintain their compliance!

7. 'My child often tantrums when I turn off his video games. Then I can't get him to do anything for me.'

    - Rather than interrupting or stopping a fun activity without notice, remember to provide advance warnings: 'In five minutes, it will be time to turn off the game.'
    - Often when children are busy watching media, playing their video games or otherwise quietly occupied, the temptation is to leave them to their devices. The parent only approaches them when it is time to turn it off. **Prepare** beforehand

and consider spending some Quality Time while they are on a device, talking about their favourite show or playing the game *with* them. Give an advance warning, and then present the transition.

› Avoid giving difficult requests immediately following a difficult transition. Instead of 'Turn off your device and do your homework', try 'Turn off your device and come and get a snack.' If they still have challenges turning off their video games, you may wish to teach them the skill of *how* to transition away from their media. We have a chapter on that!

8. 'Whenever I ask my child to do something, my spouse swoops in and does it for her.'

› This is a tough situation, to be sure. We recommend you have a private conversation with your spouse away from little ears and definitely not in the middle of your attempts to teach compliance. Discuss both of your goals. Let them know they may be undermining your child's opportunity to learn co-operation.

› Keep an open and ongoing discussion with your partner about parenting goals (in general) and how to teach compliance in particular. Suggest that they read this book with you!

9. 'I use time-outs all the time when my child is non-compliant and they just don't work.'

› When working on the skill of co-operation, Time-Out is not an effective punishment because it actually gets your child what they wanted in the first place, which is to avoid doing what you asked.

> Time-Out does not *teach* your child any skills needed for co-operation.

> Time-Out may actually be teaching your child not to listen to you! Refer back to the section on the third parenting fundamental (**Motivate**) to review the use of effective consequence strategies. And remember, most skills, including co-operation, can be learned without the use of punishment.

10. 'My child constantly receives punishment for his rude, unco-operative and argumentative behaviour. He rarely complies with our requests no matter how unpleasant we make the consequences.'

> You will remember from our chapter on 'Understanding Punishment', that it is easier and more effective to *teach* a replacement skill than to punish unwanted behaviour.

> In terms of co-operation, our approach is focused on **Preparing** your child for success, directly **Teaching** the skill and providing **Motivation** for their success. We do not advise punishing your child for a skill they may be lacking.

> And as an added bonus, you are less likely to suffer the negative side-effects of punishment: your child will not fear you or dislike you. Teaching skills is much more fun for everyone!

Let's go back to the scenario described at the beginning of this chapter. Now we know what co-operation is, what it is not and how to teach it, what could Mum have done differently to gain Scotty's co-operation?

It might look something like this:

> Knowing Scotty is playing with his favourite toys and it will be difficult for him to leave them to come to dinner, his mum decides to give him a five-minute warning. She calls up the stairs, 'Scotty!' and since they have been practising him answering when she calls him, he replies 'Ya?'
>
> She gives him the heads-up in concise language, 'Come to the table for dinner in five minutes, got it?' Scotty responds in the affirmative.
>
> Mum sets a timer so she will remember to get him once the five minutes have passed, and when it sounds, she goes up to Scotty's room. 'Okay bud. I'm going to help you tidy these toys. If you can get to the table in two minutes, then we will have time for dessert before you go to karate.' Scotty nods his understanding, but takes a full minute before he helps to clean up the toys.
>
> He complains about having to go to karate and asks why his mum even enrolled him in something he does not really like. She does not say anything in response to his comments and

7. JUST DO IT

questions, sensing they are diversionary tactics rather than reflective of a true dislike of karate. Together, they get the toys cleaned up (not perfectly, but good enough).

Scotty is at the table with fifteen seconds to spare and eats his dinner. Mum gives him a small serving of dessert. She was prepared to give him extra had he come to the table without complaint.

On the way to karate, Scotty talks about how excited he is to see his favourite instructor and to show him how he has mastered the defensive move they worked on last week. Mum opts to *not* remind Scotty about the negative comments he had made earlier about karate while he was cleaning up his toys and enjoys pleasant conversation with her son.

By using **Prepare. Teach. Motivate.** in a warm and consistent fashion, parents can teach their children to be more co-operative, resilient and likeable. Remember, all skill development takes time and practice. There will likely be many mistakes along the way. Stick to the Fundamentals and we know you will see success!

Once you have read this chapter in its entirety, you can refer to the following table for an overview of using **Prepare. Teach. Motivate.** to teach co-operation.

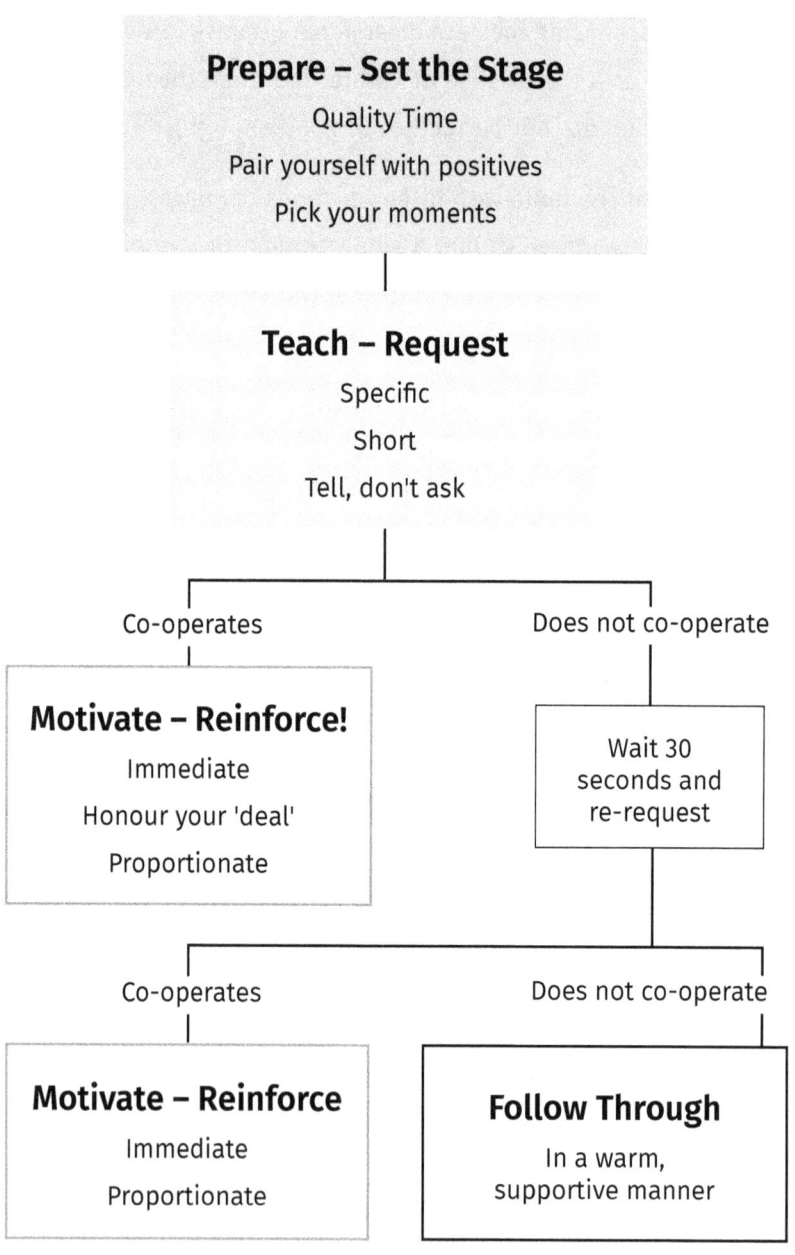

8.

You Can't Always Get What You Want:

Teaching your child to cope when you say no or ask them to wait

CAN YOU RELATE?

It's getting late on a school night, the children, adults and pets have all been fed, and homework is done. Ken and his father are winding down with a favourite book. Dad gives Ken a heads-up that he should brush his teeth and get into his pyjamas in a few minutes. A few minutes goes by, and Dad asks Ken to get ready for bed.

Ken: 'But Daaaaaaaaaad, can we read another chapter?'

> Dad: 'No, it's super late and you have school tomorrow.'
>
> Ken: 'I hate you!'
>
> Ken screams, runs upstairs, slams the door and sobs in his room, while sprinkling in some colourful language about his parents …

Does your child have difficulty when they do not get what they want, when they want? Funnily enough, so do many kids! Congratulations on being a 'Skills Detective' and noticing that sometimes our children become upset when being told no or that they are not allowed to do something.

So what are we to do?

Before you do anything, please be sure that your child has the skill of co-operation. This means that they do what they are asked, the first or second time they are asked, at least 70 per cent of the time. You might need to go back to Chapter 7 to build your child's co-operation before tackling the issue of accepting no (psst — we put these chapters in this order for a reason).

Prepare

As always, the first step when setting your kids up for success is to look for helpful **Prepare** strategies (call back to Chapter 1). In fact, for many children, consistent use of the following **Prepare** strategies is sufficient for building their tolerance to the word 'no':

8. YOU CAN'T ALWAYS GET WHAT YOU WANT

1. Have reasonable expectations. This includes reasonable expectations of what you are saying 'no' to, when you are saying 'no' and how often you expect your child to respond calmly. Be reasonable.

> **SCIENCE SIDEBAR**
>
> In 2023, Jessica VanDevander and her colleagues found that 77 per cent of neurotypical ten-year-old children calmly cope with being told 'no'. That number decreases to 70 per cent for seven year olds, then to about 50 per cent for four year olds and under.
>
> We will say it again. Be reasonable. Four year olds accept being told 'no' only about half the time. That means that half the time they are *not* calmly agreeing to your refusal to give them what they want.

2. Pick your battles … carefully. Agreeing to some, not all, of your child's requests is the best way to avoid that unpleasant tantrum. This is particularly true when your child asks for lots and lots of things and you feel like all your interactions are of you saying no and being the 'Ruiner of Fun'. Remember, it is okay to say yes at times in the service of keeping the peace and keeping everyone happy.

3. Offer choices. Rather than simply saying no, full stop, there are times when providing alternatives or options will be helpful and reasonable. Sometimes the choices are similar or fun alternatives, sometimes the other options are not as fun. Choices can be an effective way to give your child a sense of control.

CAN YOU RELATE?

Six-year-old Randall asks his dad if he can go to his friend Otto's house to play. Dad knows Otto is not available because he saw Otto leave his house with his parents.

Knowing this, and knowing there is nothing he can do to grant this request, his dad has a couple of choices:

Fun choice: 'No, Otto's out right now. Do you want to call Miles or Ella to see if you can play at their house?'

Less fun alternative: 'No, Otto's out right now. Do you want to help me make lunch or go biking together?'

Randall responds with disappointment yet calmly to the alternative, so Randall's dad validates his disappointment and gives him lots of praise. 'Randall, I see how disappointed you are that your friend isn't available. Thanks so much for being flexible. You are getting so good at that!'

Randall will be **Motivated** to accept alternatives to his requests in the future.

8. YOU CAN'T ALWAYS GET WHAT YOU WANT

4. Spell it out. When you think about it, there are a select few times that we say a definite forever NO. Most of the time we are actually saying 'not right now'. So spell it out for them. If you cannot say yes to a request, tell your child when they can have what they want. Turn the 'no' into a 'yes'. For example, if your child asks to see their grandmother when it is not possible or convenient, rather than just saying no, talk to your child about when they can or will be seeing their grandmother.

5. Provide a heads-up. Before entering a situation when you know your child will ask for something you will not be giving them, give them advanced warning. For example, when going to the store to buy a birthday present for your child's friend, you could let them know that you are buying a birthday present and will not be buying something for your child.

6. Catch them being good. As with any skill we are hoping to teach, we have to be on the lookout for when our kiddos actually tolerate being told no or not right now. When your child reacts calmly to being denied a request, make sure to notice it, comment on it and celebrate it: 'Shirley, I am so proud of you for being so calm. What a big girl you are!'

While saying 'yes' or giving choices may work to avoid some tantrums, there are many times we *cannot* avoid saying no and there may not be viable alternatives. The following requests cannot really be granted nor are there obvious choices to be offered:

» 'Dad, can I skip school today and go to the mall with my friends instead?'
» 'I don't want to wear my seatbelt.'

» 'Mum, can we get another puppy?'

Because there will always be situations in which we cannot honour our children's requests, we need to **Teach** them to accept when they cannot get what they want.

Teach

As parents, we often find creative methods to soften the blow of saying no to our children: 'I don't think so ... Let's talk about it later ... Maybe, but we'll have to see ... I'm not really sure right now.' While you think you are softening the blow, by using this strategy you are actually being unclear and sending confusing messages to your child.

Teach your child to cope with hearing no to their requests. *Kids need to hear the word 'no'.* Don't dance around it. Be clear. Be definitive. This approach is different from some parenting philosophies that advocate that parents should never say no to their child. Our approach is grounded in science, and reality. It is a *skill* to be okay when hearing the word no.

To repeat, children need to hear the word no from their parents.

No doubt, your child will hear it often in life outside your home. Teaching them to cope with the fact that you do not always get what you want will help them to navigate the worlds of school, work and society. This will **Prepare** them for those recesses when Kristy is not sharing toys, when a teacher does not let them leave for a break, when their brother is not taking turns or when the friend request they sent to that 'cool kid' is rejected.

If your child often tantrums when hearing the word no, **Prepare** by saying *yes* more often, AND, at the same time, **Teach** them by saying *no* in a more deliberate manner. A common parenting reaction to a child who really reacts to the word no, is to avoid saying no to the child altogether. While this may defuse any given situation in the short-term, it does little to build up their tolerance to being told no or being told they have to wait.

By teaching our children to tolerate no, we are equipping them to be resilient, confident and likeable when their requests are denied in the real world.

In general, remember that even when you are saying no to your child's request, you should *be nice about it*. You do not have to sound like a drill sergeant or a jail warden. Delivering your message calmly, warmly and empathetically, will be an important part of teaching them to cope with your message calmly.

Let's discuss what might happen after saying the dreaded two letters of N and O.

Teaching and Motivating Your Child to Tolerate a Clear 'No'

A recently developed approach, based in science and clinical practice, provides an excellent way to specifically **Teach** your child to tolerate no. And this approach involves … wait for it … actually giving your child what they want. This is counterintuitive and may sound as though we are contradicting ourselves about 'saying what you mean and meaning what you say', but let us explain by revisiting Ken and his request to read another chapter …

> **CAN YOU RELATE?**
>
> It's getting late on a school night, the children, adults and pets have all been fed, and homework is done. Ken and his father are winding down with a favourite book. Dad gives Ken a heads-up that he should brush his teeth and get into his pyjamas in a few minutes. A few minutes goes by, and Dad asks Ken to get ready for bed.
>
> Ken: 'But Daaaaaaaaaad, can we read another chapter?'
>
> Dad: 'No, it's super late and you have school tomorrow.'
>
> Ken: Disappointed yet calm, he says 'Fine'.
>
> Dad: 'Wow Ken. You were really calm about that. How about we read another chapter like you asked.'

Remember about finding effective reinforcers to **Motivate**? In the above example, giving a Smartie afterwards is cool, but it is *much more effective* to instead give Ken that extra reading time.

You are probably thinking, 'What do you mean you want me to give him what I just said no to?' It's an odd concept at first, but let's take a closer look.

If Ken is asking for the extra reading time, that IS the biggest, most valuable reinforcer for him at that moment. What we want to do is celebrate Ken's success at staying calm, *even after being told no*. How powerful is it if we can say to him, 'I love how you handled that and you stayed so calm. Let's read another chapter'? This will

8. YOU CAN'T ALWAYS GET WHAT YOU WANT

help him get used to hearing the word 'no'. It can be especially effective with kids who seem to instantly get upset right after they've been told no.

Now you might be thinking, 'but, in reality, we cannot always give them what they want. It's not a sustainable strategy.' If that's what you are thinking, then you're right. This is just the starting point.

There are three necessary skills to tolerating being told 'no':

1. Staying calm when *hearing the word no.*
2. Coping with *not being able to have what you would like.*
3. Figuring out *what to do* when you cannot have what you would like. This last skill is the natural precursor for developing the ability to wait for something you would like.

To teach the first of these skills, tolerating the word no by not being hair-trigger reactive, we suggest that you say it more often in *easier* circumstances. This helps your child to just get used to it. Start with things you think they will be okay with at first. You will know what is the easiest situation for your child. This might be saying no to their request to sitting in the front seat of the car, picking the song that will be playing the car or going to the bookstore. Your child needs to be okay with *hearing no to the easy things*, before hearing no to the more desirable items and activities like ice cream or the iPad.

The next step would be for your child to get some practice hearing 'no' under more difficult circumstances. When saying no to your child's request for something more important to them, *give your child* the item or activity they requested *if they remain calm*. As with the example of Ken and his dad, it might look and sound something like this: Your child requests a second cup of juice. Initially, you say no. Your child stays calm and says 'okay' or asks for water instead. We suggest you *give them the cup of juice*, along with a ton of praise for staying calm. This is a very powerful way to **Motivate** your child. They learn that 'no' is not necessarily a terrible word.

Once your child calmly accepts, the word 'no' more regularly, **Teach** towards those two additional skills needed to tolerate 'no' — not being able to have what you would like *and* knowing what to do instead.

Think about it … there are many times when you cannot have what you would like, when you would like it, and you *fill the time* with some type of activity. As adults, we have learned to wait for things. There are many everyday examples of this.

> **CAN YOU RELATE?**
>
> What you would like: To buy your groceries and leave the store.
>
> What happens: While you are standing at the checkout, the person ahead of you is counting out their change dollar by dollar, taking forrrrevvver. So you look at your phone or peruse the magazines.
>
> What you would like: For your child's tennis lesson to be completed so you can pick them up and return home.
>
> What happens: The lesson is running late by twenty minutes. So you grab a coffee.
>
> What you would like: To use the restroom at the restaurant.

8. YOU CAN'T ALWAYS GET WHAT YOU WANT

> What happens: The restroom is occupied. To bide some time, you walk around the area briefly and then return when it is vacant.

While waiting at the checkout aisle, you never know how long the wait will be. Sometimes the line or queue moves along quicker than you thought and sometimes it takes longer. Things are often unpredictable. As adults, we have learned to tolerate this unpredictability (well, at least most of us, most of the time!). When teaching our children to tolerate no, it is important to build in this unpredictability. You will see how to do this in a moment.

How do we actually **Teach** these two other skills — tolerating not getting what you want and knowing what to do when you are waiting? Let's re-visit Ken and his dad one more time. Because Ken's dad has reinforced Ken for staying calm when hearing the word 'no' on multiple occasions, Ken's dad is ready to continue teaching. The next steps are to **Teach** Ken to cope with not getting what he wants and for him to learn to occupy himself with doing other things instead. Now 'no' actually means 'no' (most of the time).

CAN YOU RELATE?

> Dad has just said 'no' after Ken asked him for one more chapter. Ken stays calm.
>
> Ken closes his book, pouts and slowly walks away. Dad then asks him to change into his pyjamas and brush his teeth.

Ken does so and Dad proudly says, 'Thanks so much for getting ready for bed. You handled that really well.'

In this example, Ken does not get what he wants at that moment. 'No' actually meant 'no'.

On occasion, when Ken asks for another chapter, his dad might say, 'Yes, but I need to get your little brother to bed first. Find something else to do for a few minutes.'

This is an example of Ken's dad throwing in some unpredictability. At the same time, Ken is learning to occupy himself while he waits for the thing he asked for. When he is successful at waiting, even for a very brief period of time, Dad congratulates his son, 'Well done Ken! Thanks for being so patient.'

Over time, we begin to teach our children to tolerate not being able to have what they would like for longer periods of time. For example, if your child asks for an ice cream, and there is none at home, they would be told 'no, we don't have any'. The following day during the grocery store run, you might buy the ice cream and offer it to your child. Praising their ability to wait for the ice cream will **Motivate** them to wait calmly the next time a similar situation arises.

One crucial thing to keep in mind … as you are teaching your child to tolerate 'no' for longer periods of time, keep going back to those early teaching steps. Sprinkle in some times when, after you've told them no and they stay calm, you then give them what

8. YOU CAN'T ALWAYS GET WHAT YOU WANT

they asked for. This is particularly important if tolerating 'no' is very difficult for your child. This unpredictability will keep your child tolerating no, within reasonable expectations, for longer periods of time.

> **SCIENCE SIDEBAR**
>
> Remember from the Reinforcement chapter ... An intermittent rate of Reinforcement, in which we provide rewards on an unpredictable schedule, is demonstrated to have longer lasting effects. Think about the bleary-eyed casino dweller who has been at the slot machine for the past five hours pulling that lever. What is keeping him there, you ask? Sometimes he wins a few coins and many, many times he does not win anything. But what he is holding out for is the Big Win! Intermittent Reinforcement is what keeps people coming back.

Now that you have gone through all the trouble of teaching your child to tolerate being told 'no', essentially you have also taught them how to 'wait' for things they want, be it your attention, a snack or another episode of their favourite show. Except for in situations of physical, moral or social peril, when you drill down, there is rarely a time when 'no' actually means 'no, never'. Most of the time when we say 'no', we are really saying 'no, not right now'. So start subbing in words and phrases like 'not right now', 'yes, a little later' and 'wait a bit'.

> **SCIENCE SIDEBAR**
>
> What we are talking about here, when we start to expand our child's tolerance to hearing the word 'no' to other words such as 'wait', 'not right now', 'in a few minutes', is an example of a behavioural principle called Generalization.
>
> In geeky behaviour terms, Generalization is when a child learns to use their skills in a variety of different settings and situations, and with a variety of different people. Behaviourists do not believe that a skill is truly mastered until it is generalized and kept over time.

Before you know it, you will have a child who copes when you tell them no, who knows how to wait, and who stays calm when they cannot have what they want.

> **PUTTING IT INTO PRACTICE**
>
> Crack open your Parenting Journal to the next available page and jot down one or two scenarios that upset your child when they are told 'no'. Also make some notes about when your child did cope with hearing, calmly, when you told them 'no' or 'not right now'.
>
> Make a few notes on the following **Prepare** strategies:

8. YOU CAN'T ALWAYS GET WHAT YOU WANT

› Do you have reasonable expectations, based on your child's age and temperament, for how often they can accept being told no?

› Did you praise, applaud or otherwise reinforce the times that your child calmly coped with hearing 'no'?

› What was it that they could not have? In general, how often do you say 'yes' to this particular request? Could you say 'yes' more often in order to avoid tantrums?

› Could you offer choices when you deny a request?

› Could you be more prepared for your child's requests and give them a heads-up if a denial is in their future?

If you have a child who really, really struggles with hearing the word 'no', consider the following ways to **Teach** them this important skill:

› What are some similar yet easier things you can say 'no' to?

› If they stay calm, can you provide the item/activity immediately after telling them no? (Hint: Initially, while teaching, you're going to do this often.)

› As they get more skilled at calmly tolerating the word 'no', can you gradually start introducing times when no really means no?

> What are some other activities they can do to fill in time while they wait for the thing they want or instead of getting the thing they asked for?

9.

Getting Out the Door:
Taking the 'mad' out of the mad dash in the morning

Weekday mornings can be one of the most hectic, most anxiety provoking and most anger-inducing times of the day. Sometimes it feels like getting your kid(s) and yourself out the door is like trying to beat a ticking time-bomb. Inevitably, you end up exhausted and stressed out before your day even starts!

It makes sense — there is not a lot of wiggle room on weekday mornings.

First, there is a hard deadline. Everyone has to be out the door by a specific time. To catch the bus. To make the bell. To be at the office. This can feel like the timer on a bomb. Beat the timer — ah, bomb defused. Miss the deadline — boom! Tears, contingency plans, perhaps even lost wages. Most of the time there is no wiggle room on this.

Second, there is a pretty specific and non-negotiable list of things to get done before that timer goes off. Clothes on. Breakfast eaten. Teeth brushed. Lunches made. Backpacks packed. Coats and shoes on. Not to mention the extras. Forgotten forms to be signed. Quick review of test material, etc., etc. Most of the time there is no wiggle room on this either.

So, let's just start this chapter with the suggestion that if you are new to teaching your child skills, do not start here. The morning routine is such a pressure-cooker situation that you may want to focus simply on the **Prepare** strategies for a while.

Do everything in your power to set your kid up for success in the morning (and yourself) by helping them with most of the routine. Help them to get dressed. Make their breakfast. Pack their bags, etc. Consider some additional **Prepare** strategies that will help for now, such as packing lunches, having weather-appropriate clothing items ready and having breakfast items on the table the evening before.

Once you have the hang of **Prepare. Teach. Motivate.** to reduce other problematic behaviours and to improve general co-operation, you are ready to tackle the morning routine. Still, consider that you will need extra time, energy and wiggle room to teach the morning routine, to wait out your child's refusals/non-co-operation, to redirect misbehaviours and to deliver on motivating rewards.

The 'morning routine' is actually a complex set of activities and choreographed dances.

The **first step** in the process of teaching your child to be independent with their morning routine will be to define what each task is. What are the tasks that *need* to get done, in what order and by what time? Be sure to define them clearly.

9. GETTING OUT THE DOOR

The routine might look something like this:

- » Get out of bed.
- » Eat breakfast.
- » Get dressed.
- » Brush teeth and complete other hygiene tasks.
- » Pack backpack.
- » Get outdoor clothes on.
- » Leave on time! (Be specific about what time you need to be out the door.)

The **second step** is to be a 'Skills Detective'. Evaluate, of these tasks, which ones your child can do on their own, or with help, or with complete assistance.

Consider whether your child needs some additional reminders for certain steps. For example, some children may benefit from having a checklist of hygiene tasks that needs to be completed (teeth brushed, hair brushed, deodorant on, medication taken, etc.). Others might need a backpack checklist (lunch, notebooks, gym clothes, etc.) or an outdoor clothing list (boots, jacket, mittens, etc.). This is where you can be very specific as to what your child needs to do depending on their age, the season or where you live. In some climates, there is a big difference between getting dressed to leave the house in January and in June. Be realistic about how long things take.

If you realize there are several tasks your child cannot yet do on their own, we suggest you teach them at another time. This chapter is about teaching them how to smoothly follow a morning routine in a timely manner that gets everyone out the door on time and with as few tears, meltdowns and/or arguments as possible.

For example, if your child cannot fully dress themselves, teach and practise this with them on the weekends and on holidays when you are both relaxed and not under time pressure. This can also be practised at times other than the mornings. Until your child is able to get themselves dressed, be there to help them get dressed on weekday mornings.

Finally, evaluate how long it takes your child to do each step.

The **third step** will be to make a visual schedule that includes the times by which each task needs to be completed. Work backwards from the time you actually have to be stepping out the door in order to get to school/work on time and assign each task a 'complete by' time.

The **fourth and final step** is to end this whole process with a reward. For example, if we can get out the door on time, we can listen to your favourite music in the car. If we can be ready by __ time, we can stop at the local donut shop for a treat. If we get out the door by __ time, you and I can play that fun version of 'I Spy' as we walk. Get creative about what will motivate your child. Mix it up and have fun!

We know that providing rewards as soon as possible after the desired behaviour is most successful in increasing the behaviour we want to see. So we do not advise you use reinforcers that can only be given after school.

After school is a long way away. Lots of road has been covered by the time they get home from school. If they earned their reward in the morning but did not receive it and then proceeded to have

9. GETTING OUT THE DOOR

a bad day, you may not feel it is 'right' to reward them. If you go ahead and give them their reinforcement, you may worry that you have reinforced the 'wrong' behaviour.

Either way, the reward will lose its power to increase the likelihood of a smooth sailing morning the next day.

PUTTING IT INTO PRACTICE

Take out your Parenting Journal and write what your child's morning routine would look like. First, fill in the time you need to be out the door. From there, working backwards, identify the times to have certain tasks completed by. Ensure the time you have written is of reasonable length.

Make a list of possible reinforcers your child can earn and get in the morning. Better yet, make the list in collaboration with your child.

Make sure these are rewards they can get/do in the morning after they have completed their tasks.

We've provided an example overleaf.

Task	Completed By
Get out of bed	7:10
Eat breakfast	7:25
Get dressed	7:35
Brush teeth and do other hygiene tasks	7:45
Pack backpack	7:50
Get outdoor clothes on	8:00
Leave on time (identified first, then work backwards)	**8:10**

Possible reinforcers: Bouncing a basketball on the way to school, listening to favourite songs, playing I Spy enroute, eating a favourite muffin.

Putting It All Together

As your child becomes more skilled at executing the various parts of the various tasks, you will start to 'fade' out your support strategies. The visual schedule for dressing may no longer be needed. The

9. GETTING OUT THE DOOR

backpack checklist gets a quick glance. But remember, you never want to fade out the reinforcement completely.

Let us repeat. You never want to fade out the reinforcement for getting out of the house on time. What you can do is switch up what the reinforcement is, and how often you give it. Now would be the time to build in surprise rewards — pizza party at the end of the week, the coffee shop stop, access to more screen time on the weekend, etc.

Voilà. Bomb defused. Everyone starts their day with a smile. ☺

10.

Giving It Up:
Teaching your child to transition away from screens

In our clinical practice, one of the most frequent concerns we hear from parents is that their kids are spending way too much time on their screens. The Xbox! The tablet! The god-forsaken phone! Just when parents get them off one screen, they find their kids glued to another one. Arguing, negotiating and managing children's screen time can be a truly endless, thankless and exhausting part of modern-day parenting.

As conscientious parents, we are well aware that screens are having an impact on our children's development and we know that excessive screen use can be problematic. There are many health professionals, researchers and parents themselves who have witnessed the damage that comes from children having too much time on their screens. We have heard that they do not develop the

10. GIVING IT UP

fine motor skills required for printing and colouring. They have shorter attention spans. Their language development is delayed. They do not know how to handle boredom. They have immature social skills and peer relations. They seem to be addicted. They are inactive, possibly obese and plagued with many associated health problems. Low self-esteem, depression, self-harm and even suicidal ideation have all been associated with social media use.

Governments around the world are working to protect the safety of our children. Australian politicians are proposing mandatory age verification to limit social media use by youth under the age of sixteen. In Canada, many school boards are instituting a complete ban on phones in the classroom. In New Zealand, there is a nationwide ban on phones in schools. The US Surgeon General wants warning labels on social media platforms to inform parents about the risks to their children's mental health. As we learn more about the long-term impacts of screen use on developing brains, we can expect to see even more rules and regulations implemented.

Some will argue that screens have their benefits. We know screens have been associated with benefits for our children's development, and that children who have zero screen time report lower mental wellbeing than those who have a moderate amount. Some video games challenge their minds and increase problem-solving. Social media helps kids stay connected with friends, even if they live far away. The internet allows children to learn and explore topics of interest.

Still, on balance, the evidence suggests that the risks of harm, especially those from social media platforms with their push notifications, infinite scroll and autoplay functions, outweigh the possible benefits. As parents, it is our job to keep our children safe, which means we have to help our children regulate their screen use.

The problem is that many of the experts in the field do not provide advice on how exactly we are supposed to manage screen time and help our kids put down their electronics. We know the fighting and negotiating is not working. And we know parents can feel very guilty and embarrassed about the state of screen time in their home.

But don't despair. There *are* ways to make screen management a less explosive issue in your home. Keep in mind, moving away from screens is a skill that can be learned. You *can* help your children develop a healthy relationship with their technology. There *will be* an end to the arguing and negotiating. This chapter will explain how to use the **Prepare. Teach. Motivate.** strategies to establish a balanced approach to technology in your home.

Prepare

Model Healthy Screen Use

Children learn so much from the behaviour of their parents. As a result, the most important first step to developing healthy technology use in our children is to model healthy screen use ourselves.

And we know, we know ... that is much easier said than done.

10. GIVING IT UP

> **CAN YOU RELATE?**
>
> Do you have the TV on even when doing other things, such as exercising, doing chores or making meals?
>
> Do you have a phone in your pocket at all times?
>
> Do you jump up from the dinner table whenever a notification pings?
>
> Do you find yourself 'doom-scrolling' while also watching Netflix with your family?

Before we can expect good screen management from our children, we may need to curb some of our own unhealthy habits. Start by taking an honest look at how often you use screen-based technology outside of what is required for your work or day-to-day chores.

Then, take steps to reduce your screen use. Put the phone down and let your kids see you engage in healthy activities such as reading, journalling, playing an instrument or practising yoga. Spend time outdoors, no matter the weather. Designate screen-free time everyday to be present and engaged with yourself, your family and your tasks.

Set Reasonable Expectations for Healthy Screen Use

Knowledge is power, and when it comes to children's screen use there are new research findings and recommendations being published every day. Screen use is a major area of concern for developmental researchers and clinical specialists. Familiarize yourself with what the world experts recommend. Try to stick to these guidelines as much as possible (pandemic parenting, sick children and unexpectedly early morning wake-ups are reasonable exceptions to the rules).

> **SCIENCE SIDEBAR**
>
> In 2019, the World Health Organization released their report, *Guidelines on Physical Activity, Sedentary Behaviour, and Sleep For Children Under 5 Years of Age.* Among many other recommendations for healthy, active living, the WHO suggested:
>
> › Children under two years of age should not have any screen time.
>
> › Children between two and five years should have only one hour of screens each day, with less being preferred.
>
> For young children, less screen use is associated with better sleep, more physical activity, improved fine motor development, better self-regulation, increased creativity and stronger communication skills.

10. GIVING IT UP

> Screen time recommendations for older children are variable, with most experts stating that children aged six–eleven years do not need their own personal devices and that their screen use (outside what is required for school) should be limited to less than two hours a day.

Make a Screen Time Contract

Sit down and collaboratively develop the rules of screen use for the family. Basic elements of the contract could include the allotted time for individual screen use per day, with weekends being different from weekdays. Then add in specifics that apply to your family. Some we like to recommend are:

- » screens are allowed during car rides that are longer than twenty minutes
- » screens are allowed only after homework is completed
- » no screens at the dinner table
- » screens are turned off at least 30 minutes before bed
- » screens live in a charging station overnight that is outside of the child's bedroom.

Be sure to add information about what will happen when the rules are followed and for when they are broken.

When rules are followed, options for Reinforcement can include a favourite activity, a fun outing, snacks or even more screen time.

Be creative and remember to use something that will motivate your child to stick with the contract for the following week.

Punishment for breaking the terms of the contract is straightforward — a penalty of lost screen time. This consequence can be very motivating.

A sample screen contract, with Reinforcement and punishment for following the contract, can be found at the end of this chapter.

Have fun developing the contract. Many kids like it to have formal 'grown-up' language that is still clear and straightforward. And be sure to have all parties sign the agreement to make it feel legitimate.

Monitor the Time. Give Warnings. And Be Ready to Catch the 'Sneaks'

The only way to be effective in monitoring our kids' use of screens is to actually monitor it. Every day. That's right ... Every. Single. Day.

When kids pick up their device, set a timer so you can keep track of how long they are watching/learning/zoning out. We want the kids to know we are going to follow-through with the rules that are laid out in the contract.

You may even consider helping them select screen activities that will fit into the allotted times. Meaning that if they have 30 minutes of screen time, we do not want them to start a two-hour movie. Or if they do start the movie, let them know that it will have to be paused at the 30-minute mark. If this seems intolerable to your child (or proves to be intolerable), help them select more time-appropriate activities (e.g., three short YouTube kids' videos).

For the tech-savvy parents, another option is to program the devices or the WiFi to cut out/turn off at a certain time. Some

10. GIVING IT UP

devices have parental controls built in to limit access to certain apps. This makes it very clear-cut and involves less in-the-moment monitoring from parents. These tools are especially useful if your child is known to be on their device at night.

As the end of the screen time approaches, give them a five to ten-minute warning. This lets the kids know you are paying attention and it helps them to get ready for the dreaded transition away.

And be on the lookout for Sneaks! Even the most angelic and honest child has been known to sneak screen time if they think they can get away with it. Sometimes children take a tablet into the bathroom with them. Some will curl up in a closet. If you notice your child has gone unusually quiet, it might be worth a quick check to see if they have tried to out-smart you. For repeat offenders, parents may need to hide devices or even lock them up.

Have Another Fun-ish Activity at the Ready

When we are first developing a child's ability to transition away from screens, we have found that we will be most successful if we have something fun (probably not as fun as screens, but still fun) for them to get into next. Having kids turn off their device and start homework will be tough for a lot of them. Have a snack ready, a magazine to look through or put on some fun music. Whatever your child might like to do for five to ten minutes before moving on will make the transition much, much smoother.

Teach

Help Them Find Other Things to Do

One of the first complaints from kids when they are told to turn off their devices is that they have 'nothing to do!' (insert dramatic eye roll here). Because they have been relying on screens for so long, especially during the pandemic, they legitimately may have forgotten about their other options. Exercise and getting outside are obviously great non-screen choices. Quiet, creative activities (such as building with Lego, reading, drawing, playing music, listening to music, colouring, etc.) are very soothing. They restore our self-regulation abilities and decrease stress in ways that screens simply do not. Face-to-face interactions with friends are also great ways to rejuvenate.

Take a few minutes to sit down with your kids and brainstorm activities they enjoy doing on their own. We have found it is more helpful to frame this around 'what we can do instead of being bored' versus 'what we can do instead of being on screens'. Post a list of all the great ideas in a place where the kids can see it.

Use Technology Together

Watching a movie, playing a video game, scrolling through social media or researching information are all ways in which we can share screen time with our kids. Shared screen time, while still not as healthy for us as exercising or creating, is a much better option than having every family member alone in their rooms on different screens. Depending on the situation, you can decide

10. GIVING IT UP

whether shared screen time is a part of the allotment outlined in your child's contract, or whether this is additional or bonus time.

Sharing screen time also gives us a glimpse into what our children are watching and to what they are being exposed. It creates opportunities to discuss important issues such as how race, violence, beauty, gender and sexual orientation are portrayed in the media, or the ways in which some technology is specifically designed to 'suck us in' and keep us playing or scrolling.

> **SCIENCE SIDEBAR**
>
> You will notice we do not refer to any particular app or platform in this discussion on screen use. There is increasing awareness of the potential harm certain social media content is having on mental health, our own and our children's. For children under the age of twelve years, we strongly recommend they do not have their own accounts that allow them to post and receive pictures and information to a wide audience. For more information, check out the US Surgeon General's advisory report, *Social Media and Youth Mental Health* (2023).

Set a time limit for shared screen use and stick to it. We want to transition away from the shared screen time in a quick and effortless fashion, to show our kids it can be done.

Teach Kids to Ask for More Time

Because transitioning from a highly preferred activity is so hard, it is okay for children to request a bit more time. Even with the contract, the timers and the warnings in place, some kids need to feel a sense of control over the end of their screen time. We have found that teaching kids to politely request a reasonable amount of time to finish up can eliminate meltdowns and upsets, especially in the early days of imposing screen limits.

Granting a request of 'five more minutes, please?' does not add much to a child's screen use, it allows them a sense of agency over the situation and it shows that we, as parents, can be flexible and reasonable. One tool to teach this skill is to remind your child — before it is time to turn off the screen and *before they have had a meltdown* — that they can *ask* for five more minutes. Our 'TEACHing' chapter under 'Teaching Functional Communication' does an excellent job of explaining this. Just be sure the screen does go off when the extra time is up.

This teaching scenario may look a little something like this:

Jessica: Happily playing video games

Parent: 'All right Jessica, five more minutes on the Playstation. Don't forget, *if you want more time you can ask for five more minutes.*'

... Five minutes later ...

Parent: 'All right, the video games are all done for tonight ... [pause]' (It's okay to remind Jessica again that she can ask for five minutes.)

Jessica: 'Can I have five more minutes, please?'

Parent: 'Absolutely, thanks for letting me know.'

As Jessica's success increases, the need for reminders decreases.

Motivate

Enforce the Screen Time Contract

Because we have already used the **Prepare** strategy of laying out the screen time plans in our collaboratively developed contract, motivation on the part of the child is already set up. But, and this is a really big but, the motivation will only be effective if parents actually dole out the rewards and punishments.

We realize this sounds like a silly thing to have to emphasize, but the biggest issue when it comes to the screen time contract is actually taking the time to enforce it. We repeatedly hear from parents that the contract does not work or that they are still fighting and negotiating with their kids to turn off the TV. When we investigate further, we find that the parents have not held up their end of the bargain by using the agreed-upon motivation elements of the contract.

We know parents are busy and they already have too many parenting issues to attend to. Yet, if we want our kids to have reasonable screen use, we will have to work at it too. Managing screens is a daily job, just like feeding and bathing.

That said, be sure to motivate your kids by finding effective Reinforcement and punishments. Feel free to look back at Chapters 5 and 6 to review how to properly use consequences (both good and bad) to motivate children to change their behaviour. When it comes to screen time, some of the most effective ways to **Motivate** children to moderate their use is to use screen time as the actual consequence.

For example, when children follow their screen time contracts Monday to Friday, they are rewarded with an extra hour of screen time on Saturday and Sunday. If they fail to follow the contract, this extra time is not given. The motivation can be built right in.

Easy peasy, right?

It sounds like it, but we know it is not always possible to stay on top of this. If you find you have slipped in terms of monitoring your children's screen use, or you have forgotten to implement the motivation strategies, don't feel bad. It happens. And the good thing is that you can re-start at any time.

Troubleshooting and Tips

1. 'After asking for five more minutes, or to finish this level/episode, my child continues to ask for more time.'

    > Consider accepting the request again — it is another learning opportunity for your child.
    > At some point, you will have to tell them that, no, they cannot have additional time and they do need to turn it off. See our chapter 'You Can't Always Get What You Want' for ideas on how to teach this skill.

2. 'I set my kid up for success just like you said to do … I used a timer. I gave them a warning. I prompted them to ask for more time. And still when the time was up, there was a nuclear meltdown.'

- › Acknowledge your child's disappointment and provide some genuine empathy.
- › Unfortunately, once they have a meltdown, you will need to ride it out. Remind your child they will have another chance tomorrow but unfortunately screen time is done for today.

3. 'Many of the games my child plays online have no clear ending point, which makes it hard to set and enforce a time limit. What do I do if my child wants to keep playing because the game is not over and she risks being banned if she leaves early?'

- › Be flexible. Try to be somewhat flexible with your expectations on the amount of time allotted on the game. The first time it happens, you may want to allow them the additional time and make a note of how long it took. The next day, remind them they will not be given the extra time to finish a game so they better pick something that won't take as long and save that particular game for a weekend when they have more screen time.
- › Be reasonable. Try to avoid asking your child to turn off the screen when they are only a minute or two away from completing the activity/video/game. Imagine how it would go over if you asked your partner to turn off the TV during overtime in the finals. It is not likely to result in their co-operation. For some kids, they are equally absorbed and committed to their screen activities.

4. 'I caught my kid watching age-inappropriate content on their device.'

   › First of all, don't freak out. Take a minute to reflect if it is age-inappropriate content, or if it is something that is disliked or not valued by the parent. While we may not agree with watching a content creator unbox toys, it may not be inappropriate.
   › If it is inappropriate, this is an excellent opportunity to discuss why the content is inappropriate.
   › Going forward, work with your child to select age-appropriate options.
   › Increase your monitoring of your child when on the screen. Consider having your child watch in a common living space.
   › Make the appropriate content *more fun*. This may be through providing them with additional time when they are selecting appropriate content, or through conversations/discussions about how fun their appropriate content show was.

Final Thoughts

Be aware that different children will have different skills when it comes to screen time management. Regardless of age, some kids become quite dysregulated when using technology, have a much harder time transitioning away from their device and are more prone to screen addiction. Others naturally manage screens in a more mature way. As such, different children may need different rules, even within the same household.

10. GIVING IT UP

Be flexible with your expectations and realize your children will change over time as they grow and mature. The screen time contract you developed for your ten year old may no longer be appropriate when they become thirteen.

Love them or loathe them, we know screens are here to stay. As parents, we have to find ways to make peace with them, enjoy their benefits, find balance for our children and keep them safe.

Screen Time Contract for [CHILD's NAME]

By signing below, I acknowledge and agree to the following conditions under which I may use my [TYPE OF DEVICE]:

1. My parents must have access to my screens and/or devices at any time and I will share my passcode with them.
2. I may use my device for a maximum of [e.g., 30 minutes] each day from Monday to Thursday.
3. I may use my device for a maximum of [e.g., 120 minutes] each day on the weekends.
4. Completing homework tasks or listening to music (with no videos) on my device does not count towards the screen time allotment.
5. My homework and chores must be completed before I can use my device for entertainment. My parents have the final say as to what is appropriate for me to watch and/or play on my device.
6. In some cases, I may not be able to use my device for the maximum duration per day. Time not used on one day may not be carried over to other days unless previously discussed with a parent.
7. My device must be turned off at least 30 minutes before going to bed and will be stored in a safe location outside my bedroom.
8. While travelling in the car, there may be times when it is appropriate to play on my device for longer durations. This must be pre-arranged with my parents.
9. I understand that failure to comply with the above conditions may result in lost access (one full day) to my device.

10. GIVING IT UP

These conditions may be modified in future with consent from all parties.

CHILD _____

PARENT _____

11.

We Can Handle This Together:
Helping your child manage their Emotions

All humans have emotions. Emotions are a normal, healthy part of being human. If we did not have emotions we would be living like robots, without experiencing pleasure, joy, anger, sadness, grief or worry.

Not only are emotions a normal and expected part of human existence, but there is also no such thing as a bad emotion. Yes, we prefer some emotions over others. We generally like to be happy instead of angry. But it is important to keep in mind that no one emotion is better or more important than any other. And nobody is 'bad' for expressing strong emotions.

11. WE CAN HANDLE THIS TOGETHER

CAN YOU RELATE?

Ten-year-old Josephine and her cousins are going on a hike with their parents. Josephine wants to take the path through the meadow but all the others want to hike the route by the waterfall. Josephine screams loudly, throwing rocks and sticks at her family, until her mother takes her back to the car for a Time-Out.

Darnel is working on his grade five maths homework and is struggling with one of the new concepts. After his grandfather attempts to help him to no avail, Darnel yells, snaps his pencil in two, crumples up his worksheet and stomps to his bedroom. He cannot be convinced to come back and try more. His grandfather lectures him on the importance of homework, emphasizing that Darnel will never get into a good college if he does not learn these maths concepts.

Sergei and his twin sister Sasha are celebrating their seventh birthday together with friends and family. Their older sister thought it would be fun to pop some of the colourful balloons that decorate the party space. Sasha was startled by the initial loud noises but was easily consoled by her father when he explained what happened. Sergei, on the other hand, cried for over 30 minutes even after his older sister stopped popping the balloons. His father took him to his room to calm down, but Sergei was not able to rejoin the party and he missed having his birthday cake.

To repeat, there is nothing wrong with any given emotion. How we express and manage that emotion is the difference between resilient, likable and successful people and those who are less so.

Learning to understand and cope with big emotions is a critical part of growing up. And, as with most skills that develop in childhood, parents have a huge influence on how well their children learn Emotion Regulation.

SCIENCE SIDEBAR

Teaching our kids Emotion Regulation is a very important parenting goal.

Consider these statistics:

> - Approximately 5 per cent of children have chronic emotion dysregulation.
> - Almost 50 per cent of children and youth with ADHD have significant emotion dysregulation.
> - Up to 62 per cent of children referred for mental health services suffer from emotion dysregulation.

And these outcomes:

> - Children who are better able to regulate their emotions tend to do better academically, even when the effects of individual IQ scores are considered.

11. WE CAN HANDLE THIS TOGETHER

> › Emotion Regulation is strongly associated with social success in the school-aged years.
>
> › Children who have dysregulated emotions are much more likely to develop psychological disorders in adulthood.

So what is Emotion Regulation?

There is no single definition of Emotion Regulation, but people generally think of it as the ability to manage emotions so that one is able to respond to an upsetting situation in a socially acceptable and effective manner and return to a state of calm in a timely fashion.

Emotion Regulation is a skill. Just like bike-riding, toothbrushing and spelling, regulating our emotions in acceptable ways is a skill all humans can learn.

In real life, expectations for socially acceptable emotional responses vary widely based on culture, age, developmental level and the situation. For example, if a two year old cries loudly when they drop their lollipop in the sand, their response is likely to be considered socially acceptable, whereas a twelve year old who has the same response would not be considered acceptable. Although if that twelve year old also had a developmental disability such as Down Syndrome, people would probably understand the response.

Another example: a ten year old who is angry and acts aggressively when losing a baseball game would probably not be tolerated, but if the same child acted angrily and aggressively while grieving the loss of a parent, they would be met with sympathy and understanding.

There are so many emotions and so many shades of colour within each.

In this chapter, our goal is to show how the **Prepare. Teach. Motivate.** framework helps kids learn the skills to handle their emotions. Most of the examples in this chapter are focused on anger, disappointment and frustration, but this framework can be applied to sadness, worry, embarrassment, jealousy and others.

Prepare

Set Realistic Expectations

As with all other skills we teach our children, we need to have realistic expectations for our child's ability to manage their emotions. Always remember that we want our children to have emotions, we want them to express their emotions and we want them to know their emotions are okay. Children do not come into this world knowing how to cope with the upsets and disappointments life will throw at them. This is a skill they will learn over time.

Moreover, all children are different. Just because your first child learned Emotion Regulation rather quickly does not mean your second child will. In general, we know that children will get better at Emotion Regulation as they get older, but even those with well-developing skills in this area may not be able to cope in particularly challenging situations. So, set reasonable expectations for your child and avoid comparing their skills to other children you know.

In addition, consider how other factors (such as fatigue, hunger, excitement, stress or illness) could affect your child's ability to cope in any given situation.

Finally, the last thing to think about when it comes to setting reasonable expectations for your child is to understand that developing Emotion Regulation is a long-game skill. It can take a long time to master. This is especially true if your child is someone who is particularly sensitive or reactive. So you might be in this for the long haul but things will get better!

Evaluate Your Own Emotion Regulation Strengths and Needs

Just like setting reasonable expectations for our children, we must be able to set reasonable expectations for ourselves. Take a moment to consider what kinds of situations you find particularly upsetting or frustrating. Maybe you struggle to regroup when there is a sudden change of plans? Are you easily irritated by sarcastic remarks from your parenting partner? Does it make you embarrassed when your child has a meltdown in public?

While considering the situations that you as an adult may struggle to cope with, also think about the ways in which you manage your emotions. Chances are, there is work to do in this area. Most of us, when we are being honest with ourselves, see that we are not always able to handle our own emotions in a socially acceptable manner. Recognizing that we are not perfect in this area (who actually is?) helps us to be more understanding of our children when they do not regulate as well as we would like.

Finally, consider how your child's emotions impact your emotions, and vice versa. Many parents notice that their children are more reactive, more demanding and less resourceful when they, the parents, are struggling emotionally. And, conversely, most of us are well-aware that our kids' reactions can push major buttons for us. Emotions do not happen in isolation. The good news is that when our children influence our emotions, we can use the opportunity to model healthy coping skills. More on that in the **Teach** section of this chapter.

Spell it Out and Provide a Heads-Up

If you think back to Chapter 1, 'Setting the Stage', you will recall that two important **Prepare** strategies are to Spell it Out and to Provide a Heads-Up.

Spelling it out means to be clear and concrete with our expectations. When it comes to Emotion Regulation, this means that we want to describe in detail what good Emotion Regulation looks like. Instead of telling our children we want them to be calm, chill or easy-going about a situation, tell them the specific behaviours you would like to see. This might mean taking deep breaths, walking away from emotionally charged situations, hugging a favourite stuffie, screaming into a pillow... whatever is considered reasonable and helpful in your home. Again, more on these specific coping tools in the **Teach** section of this chapter.

Providing a heads-up is a very powerful way to help our children regulate their emotions. Very few of us can cope well when things are thrust upon us at the last minute. If you know there is a potentially upsetting situation on the horizon for your child, a gentle heads-up

11. WE CAN HANDLE THIS TOGETHER

about what is going to happen *and what your child can do about it*, can be very effective.

Let's go back to one of the examples at the top of the chapter…

> **CAN YOU RELATE?**
>
> Ten-year-old Josephine and her cousins are going on a hike with their parents. Josephine's mother knows her daughter can be quite rigid about getting her own way in these situations, and so they talk about the different options that will be on the hike as they are driving to the park in the car.
>
> Josephine wants to take the path through the meadow but her mother suspects some of the others will want to hike the route by the waterfall. Josephine's mother explains that if more people want to see the waterfall than the meadow, then that will be the route the entire group takes. Josephine's mother explains that if that is the case, Josephine and her mother will take the meadow route the next time they come.
>
> Josephine does not like this decision and complains to her mother, but she has time to get used to the idea while in the car. When the group votes to walk by the waterfall, Josephine gives her mother a knowing look, rolls her eyes and follows along with her cousins.

Of course there will always be times when unexpected things happen. We cannot give our children a heads-up for every situation. But when we think about the coping skills of our children, the situations we are entering and possible ways to avert disaster ahead of time, we will greatly reduce the number of explosive moments.

Validate

Our last **Prepare** strategy when it comes to Emotion Regulation is to validate our children's feelings. Validation, while simple, is definitely not easy to do.

As we discussed at the start of the chapter, emotions are normal and healthy human reactions. We want our children to have emotions. We want our children to express them in ways that garner sympathy from others, rather than push others away, spark annoyance or inflame anger. While we all prefer some emotions over others, there is nothing inherently 'wrong' or 'bad' about any given feeling.

However, if we are not careful, our children will learn fairly quickly that not all their emotions are considered normal or healthy. Through our body language, words and actions, we often inadvertently give our children the message that there is something wrong with the way they are feeling. We ask our children why they are so upset. We imply they are overreacting. We tell them to just calm down. We threaten them with lost privileges when they are upset about something.

A prepared parent knows we have to accept the less-than-pleasant emotions along with the pleasant ones. And that we have to validate all our children's feelings if we want them to accept them and cope with them in healthy ways. Validation shows that we are listening, that we understand and that we are there to help.

11. WE CAN HANDLE THIS TOGETHER

Note that we can validate a person's emotions even if we do not agree with their behaviour or what led them to feel the way they do. We can validate a young child's sadness about breaking a favourite toy, even when we know it was their rough play that caused the toy to break in the first place.

So how do we actually validate our children's emotions? Here are some DOs and DON'Ts:

- » DO pause what you are doing and actively listen to what they are saying and observe how they are expressing their emotion.
- » DO get down to their level and stay close by.
- » DO be mindful of your body language. Stay calm and relaxed. Avoid eye rolls, crossed arms, heavy sighing or other signals that suggest you do not have time for this, that you do not really care or that you do not think they have reason to feel this way.
- » DO label the emotion you see. For example, a parent could say, 'I can tell you are disappointed and I can understand that.'
- » DON'T provide suggestions or solutions in the heat of the moment. Just try to understand and label your child's feelings.
- » DON'T try to negate their feelings with 'counter-arguments' (e.g., 'I think you are really smart').
- » DON'T try to 'prove' to your child that the situation did not warrant such a big reaction (e.g., 'It really wasn't that big a deal').
- » DO avoid explaining that you know just how they feel or that this happened to you when you were your child's age. The world is very different than it was twenty or 30 years ago and we do not have a full understanding of the stresses, expectations and influences impacting our children's lives. So, chances are we

really do not understand what they are going through, but we can do our best to be empathic.

Now let us revisit Darnel, his grandfather and the difficult maths homework ...

> **CAN YOU RELATE?**
>
> Darnel is working on his grade five maths homework and is struggling with one of the new concepts. After his grandfather attempts to help him to no avail, Darnel yells, snaps his pencil in two, crumples up his worksheet and stomps to his bedroom. Darnel's grandfather is frustrated with Darnel's lack of stick-to-it-iveness but realizes that now is no time for a lecture.
>
> Instead, Grandfather goes to Darnel and says, 'It looks like you are really frustrated with the maths homework.' Darnel grumbles about how all the school work seems so much harder this year and everyone else in the class is smarter than he is. Grandfather wants to reassure Darnel that he is just as smart as the others, but opts to lean into the emotions that Darnel is expressing, saying, 'It must be overwhelming to feel that way in class every day.'
>
> Darnel and his grandfather talk about these feelings. And while they do not necessarily come to a resolution about how to make Darnel feel better in class, Darnel eventually

agrees to work on his homework for another fifteen minutes to see if he can learn the concept.

Teach

Now you have begun to **Prepare** your child to have better Emotion Regulation, it is time to start teaching them the skills you would like them to have. Remember in Chapter 3, 'Being A "Skills Detective"', when we talked about finding the Positive Opposite? Teaching Emotion Regulation skills is an excellent time to do just that.

Rather than our children melting down, screaming or becoming physically or verbally aggressive, we might want them to do one of the following things:

- » Take five slow calming breaths.
- » Do jumping jacks.
- » Take a break — move away from the upsetting situation and go to a special space to calm down.
- » Engage in a distracting activity (Lego, drawing, reading, puzzles, listening to music).
- » Punch/squeeze/hug a pillow or a favourite stuffie.
- » Ask an adult for help.
- » Think logically and calmly to see the bright side of the situation.
- » Strike a yoga pose.

> » Use/repeat a personal mantra (e.g., 'this too shall pass' or 'ride the wave' or 'I wonder what my next thought will be').

And the list can go on and on. You know your child the best and you know what may work in that moment, and what may not. The key is to have a few tools your child can use to calm. No single tool will be useful in every situation.

Set a Good Example

As we have repeatedly mentioned in this book, children look to their parents to see how adults could and should behave. You have already done some thinking about your own Emotion Regulation strengths and weaknesses, and now it is time to put some good strategies on display.

Often, the best time to model positive coping skills is when we are actually *not* very upset. Find small inconveniences, upsets or nuisances throughout the day and demonstrate how you are managing them. And don't just demonstrate; talk it out and make it explicit.

> **CAN YOU RELATE?**
>
> Molly is driving her children to soccer practice when a car cuts her off. This does not actually bother her that much but she decides to take advantage of the situation to model healthy coping skills for her children.

11. WE CAN HANDLE THIS TOGETHER

> 'Hey you two, did you see what that rude driver just did? She cut me off! I am feeling very annoyed by that. I am going to take five slow deep breaths to calm myself down.'
>
> After demonstrating the deep breathing, Molly comments that she feels so much better. She is happy again and looking forward to getting to the pitch.

That said, it is also helpful to model Emotion Regulation strategies when we are actually feeling emotional. It is healthy for our children to see us having big emotions, especially if we also show them how we can recover.

Co-Regulation

Many modern parents have heard about the concept of co-regulation. Research suggests that co-regulation is the precursor to self-regulation. Before children can learn to regulate their own behaviour and emotions, they rely on their parents and other adults to help them.

From a practical perspective, all the information in this chapter is about co-regulation. A **Prepared** parent is ready to support their children through the ups and downs of daily life. They know how to **Teach** their children the necessary skills. And they also know how to **Motivate** their children to use healthy Emotion Regulation skills when needed.

For this particular **Teach** strategy, we want to spend a few minutes on how to co-regulate in the moment. This can be a powerful teaching tool.

Co-regulation in the moment means that we stay with our children when they are upset and we model some healthy strategies. We do not talk much during this time and, if we do, we use a quiet, soothing, calm tone.

We are going to go back to our third example from the beginning of the chapter, to little Sergei and his birthday party…

> **CAN YOU RELATE?**
>
> Sergei and his twin sister Sasha are celebrating their seventh birthday together with friends and family. Their older sister thought it would be fun to pop some of the colourful balloons that decorate the party space. Sasha was startled by the initial loud noises but was easily consoled by her father when he explained what happened. Sergei, on the other hand, seemed very overwhelmed and was crying loudly.
>
> Sergei's father took him to his room, where they have already set up a calming space with pillows, stuffies and puzzles. While Sergei continued to cry loudly, his father softly recited, 'I am okay. I was scared by the loud sounds but I am okay', while hugging a pillow and working on a puzzle. Every once in a while he attempted to hand a puzzle piece to Sergei. After refusing a few times, Sergei eventually came over and put

11. WE CAN HANDLE THIS TOGETHER

> a piece in place. His father rubbed Sergei's back while still quietly modelling some Emotion Regulation strategies.
>
> After about ten minutes, Sergei was calm. He went back down to the party, had his birthday cake and enjoyed the rest of the afternoon.

Note that in the above example, Sergei's father did not ask him to do anything. Nor did he discuss the details once Sergei was calm. He simply stayed with his son and modelled healthy coping (which Sergei had been practising during calm times). These simple behaviours allowed Sergei to get back to the party and re-join the fun. No fighting, lecturing or time-outs required.

Role Play and Practice

When it comes to teaching Emotion Regulation skills, we cannot just talk about them. We have to role play and practise with our children. And the only time to do this is when kids are in calm, playful or happy moods.

To repeat. We cannot practise Emotion Regulation skills in the heat of the moment. We must teach them these things when they are able to learn. Only after repeated practice and role playing will our kiddos be able to use these skills in the moment.

Role playing and practising is an excellent time to share your own experiences. Remember when we said not to tell kids we know exactly how they feel when we are validating them? That remains true. But when role playing and practising Emotion Regulation, feel free to draw on your wealth of experience. You can be playful, fun and even self-deprecating, as you role play and practise coping skills.

An important skill to role play and practise is your child being able to take a break, and eventually being able to ask for a break, when they need it. A break is meant to be a short time on their own where they can calm their emotions and settle their parasympathetic nervous system. It can be in any room or area in the home; it is *not a Time-Out. Let us repeat — It is not a Time-Out. It is not a punishment.* It is not a time for them to think about what they did wrong, what made them angry or how to 'fix' things.

When practising taking a break, *while your child is calm*, it *is* a perfect time to develop your child's Emotion Regulation toolkit. You and your child can put together a basket or box of things that are relaxing, fun and distracting. They can do any of the activities they usually like to do, within reason.

PUTTING IT INTO PRACTICE

Now is a good time to brainstorm and make notes in your Parenting Journal (yet again) …

With or without your child, think of as many Positive Opposites to fill up their Emotion Regulation toolkit for a variety of scenarios. You can draw from our list on page 235-236, but also feel free to get really creative. Nobody knows your child better than you. You will know if they are more likely to calm themselves with physical activities, creative tasks or time to read. You are the expert on your child.

11. WE CAN HANDLE THIS TOGETHER

> Review these ideas with your child and see what works for them. And then practise, practise, practise. The more often you role play and practise with your child when they are calm and agreeable, the quicker they will be able to use their toolkit when needed.

When your child becomes more skilled at taking breaks *while already calm*, you may provide them with reminders to take a break in real-life scenarios as they are beginning to unravel, become upset or escalate.

Motivate

As you are already well-aware, because you have read every single word in the **Motivate** section, the best way to encourage our children to change their behaviour is to use lots and lots of Positive Reinforcement. And, as with every skill we want our children to develop, we must make extra effort to point out when they manage their emotions well.

This means finding the small successes throughout the day on which to comment. Even if your child was highly supported and prompted, lay on the praise and rewards when they are able to regulate their emotions. Consider these examples:

» 'Gareth, you just completely ignored your little brother and walked away when he swatted at you. Well done, little man!'

- » 'Sumeet, I am so proud of how you were able to come to me for help when you were feeling frustrated with your Lego building. I am definitely able to help.'
- » 'I know you were disappointed when the snow stopped us from going to Gramma's house tonight. You did a fantastic job of managing that feeling, Pascale. Let's have a cup of hot chocolate.'

We want to really celebrate the times when our kids actually use a coping strategy we have been working on in the moment:

- » 'Zachary, I just saw you taking some deep breaths! Amazing!'
- » 'I love how you removed yourself from the argument with your brother, Hailey. That is exactly what we have been practising. Do you want to play a round of Uno together?'
- » 'Dani, I heard you screaming into your pillow a few minutes ago. Let me get you a glass of juice and we can talk about how you are feeling, if you would like.'

In general, we recommend avoiding punishment when our children display strong emotions. When we understand Emotion Regulation as a skill all kids, and adults, develop over time, then it does not seem fair to punish children for their lack of abilities in this area.

That said, parents may need to use punishment on occasion when a child's behaviour crosses the line. By this, we mean when a child hurts somebody else or damages property. When telling your child about a punishment, be sure to be clear it is the *behaviour* you do not want to see again, not the emotion. Avoid punishing a child for being angry.

11. WE CAN HANDLE THIS TOGETHER

Remember, all punishments should be mild and brief, and be mindful of the age and stage of your child. Avoid implementing a punishment when you are upset. Using **Prepare** strategies will help you and your child know ahead of time the consequences for these unwanted behaviours.

Further Thoughts

It was the goal of this chapter to provide an overview of the complicated skill of Emotion Regulation and how to use the **Prepare. Teach. Motivate.** strategies to increase your child's abilities in this area. If you find your child is not responding to these strategies, even after you have been teaching and practising for a long time, you may want to explore resources that offer a deeper dive into teaching this skill.

Some of our favourites are:

- » *Zones of Regulation* by Leah Kuypers
- » *What to Do When Your Temper Flares* by Dawn Huebner
- » *Parenting a Child Who Has Intense Emotions* by Pat Harvey and Jeanine Penzo

Moreover, you may decide to work with a mental health professional who can work with you and your child. You will need to be highly involved to help your child use what they learn in their day to day.

It is likely to be a process. Don't expect overnight results. Keep working on it. Remember, you are playing the long-game.

12.

To Sleep, Perchance to ... Actually Sleep!

Teaching your child to sleep in their own bed for the whole night

Oh, to get a good night's sleep again. A fading dream some of us have. Don't lose hope! The aim of this chapter is to help you make it a reality. Or make it a reality again. Your child's sleep may have become disrupted after a period of them falling asleep on their own and sleeping through the night.

Life happens sometimes. Factors out of our control, or even within our control, happen that interfere with our kids' sleeping on their own, through the night, in their own beds. For example:

» parenting choices (such as co-sleeping) when your kids were young seemed to fit with the family way back when, but may not make as much sense now for you or your child

12. TO SLEEP, PERCHANCE TO … ACTUALLY SLEEP!

» your child is ill and cannot fall asleep, so you agree to lie in their bed with them to soothe them until they fall asleep or come to them when they wake up in the night
» your child has night terrors or nightmares that compel you to go to them in the night
» a relative has an extended stay and ousts your child from their room to bunk with a sibling
» a parent is away for extended periods for work so there is a free space in your bed (and you enjoy the closeness of sleeping with your child).

None of the above situations are 'wrong' or 'bad' or 'detrimental' to the wellbeing of your child in general … unless their sleep is disrupted, your sleep is disrupted and nobody is getting the sleep they need or want. Then it may be time to consider a change. If, as a parent, you enjoy sleeping with your child, do not mind being available to your child in the night to help them fall back to sleep and/or believe a co-sleeping or family-bed arrangement is the best one suited for your family, carry on. No judgment here. Skip this chapter.

In this chapter, we will show you how to teach your child to:

1. fall asleep on their own
2. sleep through the night
3. stay in their own bed.

> **SCIENCE SIDEBAR**
>
> According to Health Canada (2019):
>
> › one in three children have trouble going to sleep and staying asleep
>
> › one in five children have difficulty staying awake during the day
>
> › one in ten children do not find their sleep refreshing.
>
> Research has shown that disrupted, interrupted and insufficient sleep leads to all sorts of daytime problems with mood, behaviour and even learning in children.
>
> In toddlers, insufficient or poor quality sleep can set your child up for increased and prolonged tantrums.
>
> In school-aged children, poor sleep has also been associated with difficulties learning and trouble regulating their emotions like frustration, sadness and anger.
>
> And in teenagehood, poor sleep is ever-increasingly associated with mood and mental health problems.

12. TO SLEEP, PERCHANCE TO … ACTUALLY SLEEP!

Anatomy of a Good Night's Sleep

Before we go much further, here's a quick primer from the National Sleep Foundation on what happens in our brains and bodies when we sleep (www.sleepfoundation.org).

Generally, when left to our own devices, our bodies and brains fall into a pretty regular pattern of sleep cycles. Each sleep cycle is divided into characteristically different stages of sleep:

- » Stage One: The 'Cat Nap'. This is the brief period when you are falling asleep. It is a very light sleep during which your brain stays somewhat alert and when you can be easily woken. When you take a five to ten minute cat nap, your brain and body are in Stage One of the sleep cycle.
- » Stage Two: The 'Power Nap'. This stage is also characterized as a 'lighter' sleep, although deeper than the cat nap stage. When you want to take a power nap, you will want to wake yourself up before the end of Stage Two (about twenty minutes).
- » Stages Three and Four: 'Deep Sleep' and 'Dead Asleep'. These stages are the 'deep' and 'deeper' sleep cycles. It is somewhat harder to rouse from Stage Three sleep and you'd likely feel quite groggy and disoriented if you were. It's even harder to rouse from Stage Four sleep. It is the 'dead to the world' stage when the fire alarm could be going off and you would be less likely to wake up. This is an important time of sleep for our bodies — it is the time of muscle and tissue repair, of growth and immune function and of replenishing our proverbial gas tanks.

> REM Sleep: 'Dream Sleep'. This is the time for the brain to do its thing to consolidate memories and learning, to transfer learned information into our file storage systems (long-term memory stores) and it is the time when we dream. It usually takes about 90 minutes to cycle through the first four stages and get to a REM stage. As the night goes on, while it still takes about 90 minutes to get there, we spend more and more time in REM with each successive cycle. We can spend up to an hour at a time in REM sleep.

By the time kids are school-aged, most of them are sleeping in 90 to 100 minute cycles. Our sleep is 'thinnest' or lightest as we transition back through to Stage One sleep. This is the time when we are most vulnerable to waking up briefly to roll over, fluff the pillow and ideally go back to sleep.

Nighttime Routines

Thinking back to **Prepare**, you already know it is important to set our kids up for success, and that certainly applies to sleeping as well. In that vein, the single-most important **Prepare** strategy for sleep is to develop a nighttime routine that is as pleasant, relaxed and as consistent as possible. A nighttime routine could include some or all the following:

> Having a specific time in mind for when you want to start the routine and a time you would like your child to be in bed for the night.

12. TO SLEEP, PERCHANCE TO … ACTUALLY SLEEP!

- » Turning off electronic devices, televisions, etc., at least 30 minutes before lights out.
- » Removing electronic devices, televisions, etc., from bedrooms.
- » Dimming the household lights.
- » Eating a small snack (being careful the snack does not contain caffeine or chocolate) at least 30 minutes before lights out.
- » Having a bath or shower.
- » Changing into comfortable pyjamas.
- » Brushing and flossing teeth.
- » Reading a book in bed.
- » Doing mindful meditation in bed.
- » Tucking into bed and saying goodnight.
- » Turning out the lights.

For some children, a reliable and predictable bedtime routine is all that is needed to get them on track (or back on track) for a good night's sleep. If you implement a bedtime routine consistently for two or three weeks and see no progress in your child's abilities to fall asleep on their own, and to stay in their bed asleep for the entire night, then you may want to consider the information below.

Sleep Dependencies

We all have things we like to have with us when we sleep or like to do to help ourselves fall asleep. We have a favourite pillow, enjoy reading a few pages of a book or relax our bodies with yoga stretches. Over time, these things become associated with falling asleep or getting us into Stage One. Other examples include listening to soft music, listening to deep breathing meditation or progressive muscle relaxation exercises ... any part of the routine that is done right before falling asleep.

Interestingly, when we wake up briefly in the middle of the night as we end one sleep cycle and head back into the next, we are more likely to 'roll over and go back to sleep' without even being aware ... if all the same conditions are present as when we went to sleep. As an adult, if you usually fall asleep at night while you are reading, you may find yourself up in the night reading a page or two just to get back to sleep. All these things we rely on to help us get to sleep are called Sleep Dependencies.

> **SCIENCE SIDEBAR**
>
> Although we may not realize it, sleep researchers have long known that we as adults wake up many times during the night and often quickly fall back asleep, since our sleep dependencies are still there. Similarly, children will wake up many times during the night between sleep cycles. If their environment is similar to how they fall asleep, they quickly return back to sleep.

Sleep Dependencies are not in and of themselves a problem. In fact, they are a critical **Prepare** strategy. What becomes problematic is when the things you depend on, or associate with falling asleep, are not there when you wake up during the night. Or when the

12. TO SLEEP, PERCHANCE TO … ACTUALLY SLEEP!

things that you associate with falling asleep are suddenly removed or inconsistently available.

> **CAN YOU RELATE?**
>
> Each night, you watch television in bed while eating a bedtime snack. Knowing you will probably fall asleep with the television still on, you set a timer for it to turn itself off in an hour when you are sure you will be fast asleep. Then, more nights than not, you find yourself up about two hours later, unable to fall back asleep, wandering down to the kitchen for a snack, crawling back into bed and reaching for the remote.
>
> As a toddler, Ramona loves to fall asleep with her mother lying by her side. She enjoys the warmth of her mother's body, pressed up against her, as she drifts off to 'La-la-land'. Ramona's mother quietly slips out of her daughter's room when she is sure Ramona is asleep, about 30 to 40 minutes later. While Ramona's mother enjoys these times of quiet closeness with her daughter, the problem comes at 1 o'clock each morning. Ramona calls out for her mother to return to her bed or crawls into bed with her mum and dad to fall back to sleep pressed up against her mother's cozy body. Ramona's mum cannot remember the last time she herself got a full night of uninterrupted sleep.
>
> Murray, on the other hand, is excellent at going to sleep on his own. His nighttime routine includes falling asleep on

> the couch, listening to the soothing sounds of his favourite cartoons on low volume. When his parents are sure that he is asleep, they turn off the TV and carry him to his bed. His parents realize there is a problem when they are awoken in the night by the sound of the TV and Murray happily watching television at 3 o'clock in the morning.

In the examples above, sleep either becomes interrupted or delayed. When sleep gets interrupted or falling back to sleep is delayed, the adult or teen has the sense that it 'took them forever to fall asleep', that they 'were up all night' or that they 'had a fitful sleep', etc. The child, who may not be as insightful, may be grumpy, irritable and difficult to get going in the morning.

Ideally, you want to fall asleep under conditions that will be pretty much the same as when you wake up in the night. Then you will likely 'roll over and go back to sleep' within seconds or minutes. We want the same for your children.

> Let's illustrate this with a couple of examples. In both cases, there are two sleep dependencies: the sound machine and the weighted blanket.
>
> Fall asleep with the sound machine (on a timer) and weighted blanket -> Wake in the night when the sound machine has turned itself off:

12. TO SLEEP, PERCHANCE TO ... ACTUALLY SLEEP!

> **RESULT:** Cannot easily fall back to sleep.
>
> Fall asleep with the sound machine (no timer) and weighted blanket -> Wake in the night with the sound machine still on, but blanket is on the floor:
>
> **RESULT:** Pull up blanket and easily fall back to sleep.

Parents need to identify those sleep dependencies that may be interfering with their children's good night's sleep. Common examples include falling asleep:

- » with the TV or radio on
- » while reading books
- » with bottles in bed
- » with toys in bed
- » with a 'full belly'
- » with the presence of another person
- » while being rocked or patted
- » with lights on
- » with a blanket, stuffie or pacifier that can fall out of bed.

The good news is that by being a good 'Skills Detective' (remember Chapter 3?), parents can also identify replacements for these dependencies and they can re-**Teach**. Children can be taught to fall asleep with things that don't require parent presence, with things that can be there in the middle of the night, and with things that are transportable (for those times when the child has to sleep away from home). For example, sound machines on continuous play tend to work well to replace things like TV, radio, cause and effect toys, etc. If your child must have a light on, a small nightlight with a red bulb is a good choice, as red light does not interfere with sleep quality in the same way blue or yellow light does.

Remember, the goals of this chapter are for your child to:

1. fall asleep on their own
2. sleep through the night
3. sleep in their own bed.

Achieving these goals really comes down to mastering the first step. Once your child is able to fall asleep on their own, the rest follows logically. In order to teach your child to fall asleep on their own, it is important that the child goes into bed and the parent *leaves the room before the child falls asleep.*

If your child has multiple ineffective sleep dependencies, you may want to fade them out gradually or sequentially eliminate them one by one, until you are at a point where only the effective ones remain.

The HOW TOs of Sleep Training

Prepare

1. Make sure the bed is for sleeping ONLY. Break the habit or, better yet, do not get into the habit of doing things in bed

12. TO SLEEP, PERCHANCE TO … ACTUALLY SLEEP!

during the day that are not related to falling asleep. This means not watching screens in bed, doing homework in bed or snacking in bed. We want our children to associate going to bed with falling asleep.

2. Make sure your child's room is conducive for sleep. The room should be cool, darkened or dimly lit and quiet with constant low-volume background noise or no noise at all.
3. Pick a bedtime. During this period of teaching, 'lights out' should be about 30 minutes later than your child typically falls asleep right now. This is to ensure they are actually tired or more tired (but not overtired) when you want them to fall asleep.

Remember, **Prepare** strategies set up your child for success. If you turn the lights out when their body is more ready to fall asleep, they will be more likely to fall asleep and have success … ahhh Reinforcement! Sleeping feels good. This should in turn increase the likelihood of them falling asleep again at bedtime.

Delaying their bedtime by 30 minutes can be temporary. Once the new skill of falling asleep on their own and in their own bed is established, you can slowly pull the bedtime earlier in small five to ten minute increments until it is at a time where they are getting enough sleep for their age. See the chart at the end of the chapter that gives the approximate amount of sleep children should be getting at each age.

4. Be sure to give yourself plenty of time before 'lights out'. Give everyone enough time so bedtimes are relaxed and enjoyable routines rather than rushed, naggy and full of fights and tears.

5. If part of your child's difficulty going to sleep independently is that they want your attention or to interact with you, make sure you provide them with lots of attention, quiet 'Quality Time', reading, listening to music together, doing a guided meditation, etc., as part of the bedtime routine *before saying goodnight*. If your child likes to play with a particular toy, have them play with it as part of the routine* and then put it away or give it to you *before saying goodnight*. Make sure your child has had their last glass of water, their last visit to the toilet and their last kiss goodnight from anyone not engaged in the bedtime routine *before saying goodnight*.

Teach

Once you complete your bedtime routine (see above for examples) and you leave your child's room, it is time to pull out **Teach** strategies.

Before continuing down this path of sleep training, consider the timing of what you are getting yourself into. Choose your timing wisely. Be honest and select a time that you are most likely to be able to stick with until sleep habits are back on track. As you will see, in the early stages of sleep training, while you are teaching your child to sleep more, you will likely be sleeping less. Remember, this is temporary. It's best to select a start time when you and your child can tolerate less sleep. This might be during the school holidays when you are at home and have a more flexible schedule, or another time when you have fewer work and home commitments.

---

*(unless of course it is screen-related because then it should be long since turned off)

12. TO SLEEP, PERCHANCE TO … ACTUALLY SLEEP!

And we get it … this is the hard part … you may need to tolerate listening to your child cry, scream or even beg you to come back into the room as soon as you leave. Please hold your judgement and read to the end of the chapter. Notice that the early stages of teaching will only require you to tolerate those behaviours for seconds at a time, if at all. Through this process, your child will learn that you come back … you always come back.

> **SCIENCE SIDEBAR**
>
> You may have heard of 'Ferberizing'. This term likely conjures up many unpleasant images of listening to babies cry for hours on end. Dr Ferber's approach has been widely misinterpreted as simply letting your child 'cry it out' in a cold and distant manner.
>
> In fact, his approach involves systematically visiting your child once they start crying to provide quick check-ins and reassurance. We suggest a slightly different, yet similar approach, based on research by our colleague, Dr Greg Hanley, one that has you visit your child regardless of whether they are crying or not. In fact, the goal is to visit them *before* they start crying. By using a process of Progressive Waiting, your child learns to fall asleep without you. They are no longer using your presence as a sleep dependency.

We recommend using a process of Progressive Waiting to delay your usual response to an interfering behaviour in small and predictable increments. By interfering behaviour, we mean those behaviours that are interfering with your child rolling over and falling back to sleep without calling out, crying, screaming or getting out of bed to seek you out.

The schedule below is our take on Progressive Waiting, which we developed based on Dr Ferber's seminal work in 2006, the researchers who have since adapted it and our clinical experience:

Day	At first wait	Second wait	Third Wait	Subsequent visits
1	1 minute	2 minutes	3 minutes	3 minutes
2	2	3	5	5
3	3	5	7	7
4	4	7	10	10
5	6	9	12	12
6	8	12	16	16
7	10	15	20	20

This is a process of undoing the accidental association between the unwanted behaviour (calling out for you, crying in the night, wandering into your bed) and the Reinforcement that has come to be associated with it (one more hug, your warm bed, another snack).

12. TO SLEEP, PERCHANCE TO … ACTUALLY SLEEP!

The way this works is that you leave your child's room while they are awake and presumably they do what it is they do to make you return (cry, call out, scream). But this time, instead of responding to their behaviour (the one you don't want to see anymore), what you are going to do is stick to a schedule to tell you when to return to them.

So two things could happen … Your child does not call out before the first interval is up. You go in anyway and say goodnight or kiss them on the cheek. The other thing that could happen is that they immediately cry or call out or try to leave their room. You wait outside their door and only go in after the set interval. So whether they call out for you or not, you will return when the silent timer tells you to. Not when your child does (or does not, as in the first case).

Rest assured we are not advocating abandoning your child at night or leaving them to 'cry it out'. We are recommending you break the contingency or association between their behaviour (calling out, crying, screaming) and your behaviour (calling back, bringing water, crawling into bed with them) while still being responsive to their need for you to come to them.

When you go in for a visit, spend only one to two minutes in their room. During this time, rub their arm or back, adjust their blanket if needed, give them a kiss on the cheek and provide other reassurances. After a minute or two, give them a final kiss or pat and say goodnight. Then leave the room. Period. Leave the room.

It is critical at this point that you DO NOT lie down with them, that you DO NOT pick them up and that you DO NOT restart the bedtime routine.

After saying goodnight, you will leave the room whether your child is relaxed or not, even if they are upset, crying or asking you to come back. We know this can be very difficult to do. Remember, your child is safe, warm, full and has had lots of your attention before saying goodnight. Now is the time to teach a new skill. We are trying to teach them that their crying is not the thing that is getting you back in the room. We are teaching them that you will come back in the room and are not abandoning them in their time of need.

Now that you understand how to do the visits, follow the Progressive Waiting schedule. As you can see, the idea is to continue increasing the time between visits in very small increments.

Let's walk through the first night of 'sleep training':

Step 1: After saying goodnight to your child, you will check-in after one minute. Provide comfort, reassurance, say goodnight again. Leave the room and set the timer for two minutes.

Step 2: After two minutes, go into the room and check-in, *whether your child is crying or not*. If they are awake and not crying they will be glad to see you have come in anyway and will learn to trust that you come back. Re-set a timer for three minutes.

Step 3: Lather. Rinse. Repeat. Until your child is soundly asleep.

On the first day, after you've done your check-ins after one, two, and three minutes, keep checking in every three minutes, until your child is soundly asleep (hopefully for the night!).

During these check-ins, don't worry about waking them up; if they have by chance fallen asleep, give them a light peck on the cheek and leave the room.

Step 4a: If your child wakes up within the next two hours, do a check-in and keep your timer set for three minutes.

12. TO SLEEP, PERCHANCE TO … ACTUALLY SLEEP!

Step 4b: If your child sleeps for two hours or more and then wakes up calling for you, begin your intervals where you started that night. If it's the first night of 'sleep training' set your timer to check-in at one minute, then two minutes, then three minutes and keep it at three minutes until they are back to sleep … hopefully for the night.

Motivate

Have a conversation with your child about the things that are naturally motivating about falling asleep on your own, in your own bed, for the whole night. It's a sign of growing up. It's good for their body and mind. It allows them to go to sleepovers at a friend's house. They will be ready to go to a sleep-away camp with their friends.

It is okay to explain the whole procedure to your child, let them know you will 'come and check on them' regularly and you are not ignoring them.

When it comes to learning the skill of sleeping independently, the natural motivator is actually the sleep! Just as having a snack when very hungry, nothing feels better than being tired, falling asleep quickly, sleeping through the night and feeling rested and energized the next day. Over the course of sleep training the goal is for your child to use their new dependencies in place of their previous ones, while still having a good night's sleep. By the end of the training, the sleep with their new dependencies (e.g., sound machine, favourite stuffie) is just as good as it was with their old dependencies (e.g., Dad, the TV playing). Voilà — sleep is still reinforcing.

As an added measure, be sure to celebrate your child's successes in the mornings during sleep training. Hopefully, you will see substantial improvements in their ability to fall asleep on their own almost every day, so be sure to tell them how proud you are, with genuine enthusiasm. Your assurances that they are doing a good job will **Motivate** them to continue to work on this goal.

Don't forget that you also need some motivation to stick with this. We know it can be gruelling to start that sleep schedule over again, from the first one-minute interval at 2 o'clock in the morning when all you want to do is bring them into your bed and get back to sleep. Your reward, your motivation for sticking this through, is the uninterrupted good night's sleep you will be able to get (again) when this skill is mastered.

Final Thoughts

Quality sleep is absolutely essential for all humans in order to function effectively in our day-to-day lives. Being able to fall asleep on our own and sleep through the entire night are skills just like any other: for some children these skills develop naturally but others require more help to get there. There are many, many strong opinions about the best approach to teaching the skill of sleep to our children. In our experience, with our own children as well as those with whom we work, the skill of sleep is best developed using **Prepare. Teach. Motivate.** It is a kind, consistent and evidence-based approach that can be effective in a fairly short period of time.

Teaching sleep skills to a child who has developed a passionate attachment to an interfering sleep dependency can be tiring and

12. TO SLEEP, PERCHANCE TO … ACTUALLY SLEEP!

challenging. We know it is hard to be consistent when you are exhausted yourself. We have been there. Yet we guarantee that following the principles outlined in this chapter will be well worth it. Having children sleeping independently can be a complete game-changer for them and for their parents.

If you encounter hurdles during your journey of teaching sleep independence, please check out the following trouble-shooting section.

Trouble-Shooting

1. 'This is all well and good but I can't keep my child in their room. She gets out of bed and leaves her room to come and find me.' If your child is one to leave their room, there are a few different things you could do:

    › If this happens immediately after you have put them to bed and they have not slept at all yet, you will be sitting in or by their doorway. You will be there to guide them back to bed before they even leave their room.

    › You could consider installing a baby gate that would block them from leaving. If they are small enough not to climb over it, they would likely stand at the gate and cry or call out for you. You would wait for the interval to be over to do your next 'check-in', guide them back to their bed, give them a pat and a kiss goodnight, leave and start the next interval.

    › With the above strategies, it will be imperative that you DO NOT talk to your child about getting back to bed, DO

NOT try to convince them how warm and snuggly their bed is and DO NOT cajole them into returning to bed. Guiding them back to their bed happens calmly, without talking to them and with a gentle hand.

2. 'My child is physically aggressive, struggling and resisting returning to their bed and I end up wrestling with them and carrying them back to their bed. Then I end up having to hold the door closed.'

   › You don't want to wrestle with them. If your child tries to duck and run away, you don't want to make it a game of chasing them around the house. You really don't want to have to pick them up either.

   › We suspect there may be a problem with daytime co-operation. If this is happening, honestly evaluate if your child actually co-operates with you at other times of the day. This will be a skill they MUST have *before* addressing sleep and challenges at night for the reasons mentioned above. See Chapter 7 for a refresher on how to gain co-operation during the day.

   › It is extremely important that parents do not resort to locking children in their rooms at night, or at any other time for that matter. This could be very dangerous in an emergency or misused by a sibling or sitter. Moreover we want our children to associate their bedrooms with positive experiences.

12. TO SLEEP, PERCHANCE TO ... ACTUALLY SLEEP!

3. 'I went to check on my child at the fourth interval and he had fallen asleep on the floor. He looked so uncomfortable and cold. I felt like such a horrible parent. I didn't know if I should wake him up to put him to bed or not.'

    › Our advice would be to leave your child to sleep there. You could tuck a blanket around him if you think he is cold or perhaps slide a pillow under his head. But the reality is, if he is really that uncomfortable, he will make his way back to his bed himself and hopefully roll over and fall back to sleep.

    › Should he go back to bed and then call out, you go back to using your scheduled 'check-ins'.

4. 'Our son quickly learned to sleep on his own with the Progressive Waiting technique. It has brought so much calm to our home. The authors of this book are miracle workers! Our challenge is that he has started having nightmares and we don't know what to do. We want to comfort him but we don't want to sabotage all our hard work!'

    › Congratulations on sticking it out and reaping the benefits of sleep training! We definitely do not want to have some pesky nightmares interfering with your great progress.

    › First of all, nightmares are a common phenomenon in children. They do not necessarily mean your child is stressed, worried or upset about something. Bad dreams just happen sometimes.

- When they occur, check on your son in a calm and caring manner, with the goal of getting him back to sleep as quickly as possible.
- Keep the lights off or low, offer some comfort, set up the sleep dependencies if they have been disrupted, tuck him back in and leave the room.
- Do not prolong the disruption by asking questions about the dream, engaging in long and drawn out 'monster-checking' around the room or offering to set up watch at the door. Get in and get out as quickly as you can.
- For parents who are in the midst of the sleep-training process, be mindful that your child may be calling for you and/or reporting they've had a nightmare as a way to get you back in the room. If they have woken up and are calling for you because they have had a nightmare, go to them to provide (brief) comfort, tuck them back in and re-set the timer.

5. 'My child was just falling asleep and then the timer woke him up!'

- There are many free vibrating timer apps for mobile devices to help with sleep training. Some even have a dark mode.

6. 'My child wet his bed during the Progressive Waiting. What do I do?'

- Not a problem. Calmly change your child and the sheets, provide some comfort, tuck them in and say goodnight.

12. TO SLEEP, PERCHANCE TO ... ACTUALLY SLEEP!

> Continue as you have been with the Progressive Waiting schedule.

7. 'I haven't seen any improvement. My child screams right away after I leave the room and they are crying inconsolably.'

    > We get this question A LOT. It can be very discouraging to feel as though your child has made no progress, even though you have followed the plan to the letter. Before throwing in the towel, we ask parents to first explain to us what they mean by 'no improvement'. Your child may still be crying inconsolably, but are they actually falling asleep any earlier? This would be considered progress! Are they crying less, but calling out instead? This would be considered progress, as well! Are they sleeping more? Progress!

    > If you truly haven't seen any improvement after implementing the sleep training correctly for three days, something needs to change.

    > It is likely the intervals between your check-ins are too long. Remember, the suggested Progressive Waiting schedule is a guideline, and could be adjusted for each child. We've included a sample schedule.

    > For children who are highly sensitive to their parent leaving the room, the first check might even be as quick as five seconds, instead of one minute. Then the second and third checks are also shorter, such as ten and 20 seconds in between. Even if it's a *gradual* change, it's still an improvement.

> In this case you are trying to get that first visit in before they are crying. Keep to your shortened interval schedule and carry on.

> If adjusting the schedule, the most important factor is that you gradually increase the time between check-ins, so your child learns to fall asleep on their own.

If after five days there is no improvement at all, consider taking a break from sleep training for several weeks (or months). Remember to adjust or tailor the schedule to your child's needs once you are ready to re-start.

How much sleep is enough?

The Canadian Pediatric Society recommends parents follow these guidelines published by the Canadian Society for Exercise Physiology (CSEP) in their Canadian 24-hour Movement Guidelines that were released in June 2021. These were the most recent guidelines at time of publishing.

12. TO SLEEP, PERCHANCE TO ... ACTUALLY SLEEP!

Age	Number of hours of sleep
1 to 2 years old	11 to 14 hours (good quality sleep, including naps and consistent bedtimes and wake-up times)
3 to 4 years old	10 to 13 hours (good quality sleep, which may include naps, with consistent bedtimes and wake-up times)
5 to 13 years old	9 to 11 hours (at night with consistent bedtimes and wake-up times)
14 to 17 years old	8 to 10 hours (at night with consistent bedtimes and wake-up times)

Sample Progressive Waiting Schedule

After you say goodnight to your child, should they call out, cry, scream or attempt to leave their room, use the guide overleaf to gradually and systematically increase the time between your visits until your child falls asleep (or falls back to sleep):

Day	At first wait	Second wait	Third Wait	Subsequent visits
	(30 seconds)	(1 minute)	(2 minutes)	(2 minutes)
1	1 minute	2 minutes	3 minutes	3 minutes
2	2	3	5	5
3	3	5	7	7
4	4	7	10	10
5	6	9	12	12
6	8	12	16	16
7	10	15	20	20

Concluding Remarks

We hope this book has given you a solid foothold in the fundamental principles of **Prepare. Teach. Motivate.** We have worked with many families over the years and, no matter what the problem or concern, we consistently return to these three basics when we develop solutions for children's behaviour.

We are deeply honoured by the opportunity to share our insights with you in *Complex Kids, Simple Solutions*. We are encouraged by your optimism to pick up this book, to persevere and to continue to make positive changes in the quality of your family's life.

That said, should you find your child's challenging behaviours do not relent, or possibly even get worse, with the consistent application of these strategies, we encourage you to seek professional help from a Child Psychologist or Behaviour Analyst in your area.

Behaviourally minded and well-informed parents are a true pleasure to work with. Often it is just a matter of 'tweaking' the parenting approach to generate success. And for those children who need a more in-depth approach, please know that you have already laid a solid foundation by utilizing our **Prepare. Teach. Motivate.** strategies.

Good luck on your parenting adventures.

May your children all develop into resilient, confident, likeable humans.

Acknowledgements

We are extremely grateful to the thousands of children, youth and families that we have had the privilege to work with, learn from and grow with over the many years of our clinical practices. We continue to be truly humbled and impressed by people's capacity for kindness, fortitude and growth. Many of the children, youth and families we know face significant obstacles in their day-to-day lives and we sincerely appreciate their trust in us. We look forward to many more years of collaboration.

We are deeply indebted to the wonderful staff at Exisle Publishing who, for reasons we can still not fully comprehend, took a chance on three unknown Canadians and our little book. Many, many thanks to Anouska, Gareth, Nathan and the rest of the Exisle gang, and to our editor Madeleine. You all helped us to **Prepare** this book to be the best it could be, you were able to **Teach** us the complexities of publishing, and you **Motivated** us with your sincere praise and enthusiasm. We could not have asked for a better team.

We would like to give a shout out to the extraordinary people who have mentored us along the way. Professionally, we have learned so much from Dr Adrienne Perry, Dr Jennifer Dunn Geier and Dr Greg Hanley and we would like to thank them for fostering environments from within which we were encouraged to learn and grow. Personally, we would like to acknowledge our parents, stepparents, aunts, uncles and grandparents who have unknowingly shaped our **Prepare. Teach. Motivate.** philosophy. We hope that this book is an adequate representation of your combined wisdom and guidance. If you disagree with anything we have written, we look forward to hearing your feedback. ☺

And finally, we are each truly fortunate to have had the loving and unconditional support from our immediate families through this long writing process. Thank you to Scott, Otto and Sam, Mary, Mia and Theo and Andrew, Sam and Lucy for tolerating our many absences for 'book club' meetings, for looking through early drafts with kind yet critical eyes and for never, not once, telling us to give it up. Thank you does not even come close to cutting it. You are the most resilient, confident and likeable people we know.

References

Baldwin, J. D., & Baldwin, J. I. (2000). *Behavior principles in everyday life* (4th ed.). Pearson.

Barkley, R. A. (2020). *Taking charge of ADHD: The complete authoritative guide for parents* (4th ed.). The Guilford Press.

Canadian Society of Exercise Physiology. (2019). *Canadian 24-hour movement guidelines*. https://csepguidelines.ca/

Compass Health Center. (2024). *Behavioral dysregulation in children*. https://compasshealthcenter.net/specialties/dysregulation-in-children/

Crowell, S. E., Puzia, M. E., & Yaptangco, M. (2015). The ontogeny of chronic distress: Emotion dysregulation across the life span and its implications for psychological and physical health. *Current Opinion in Psychology, 3*, 91–99. https://doi.org/10.1016/j.copsyc.2015.03.023

Doran, G. T. (1981). There's a SMART way to write management's goals and objectives. *Journal of Management Review, 70*, 35–36.

Ellehauge, E., Thoustrup, C., Nielsen, M. N., Pagsberg, A. K., & Hagstrøm, J. (2023). Frequency and types of emotional dysregulation in referrals to child and adolescent mental health services. *Acta Psychiatrica Scandinavica, 148*(2), 165–178. https://doi.org/10.1111/acps.13544

Ferber, R. (2006). *Solve your child's sleep problems*. Simon & Schuster.

Ghaemmaghami, M., Hanley, G. P., & Jessel, J. (2016). Contingencies promote delay tolerance. *Journal of Applied Behavior Analysis, 49*(3), 548–575. https://doi.org/10.1002/jaba.333

Ghaemmaghami, M., Hanley, G. P., & Jessel, J. (2021). Functional communication training: From efficacy to effectiveness. *Journal of Applied Behavior Analysis, 54*(1), 122–143. https://doi.org/10.1002/jaba.762

Gover, H. C., Hanley, G. P., & Ruppel, K. W. (2022). On the generality of preference for contingent reinforcement. *Journal of Applied Behavior Analysis, 55*, 318–336. https://doi.org/10.1002/jaba.892

Graziano, P. A., Reavis, R. D., Keane, S. P., & Calkins, S. D. (2007). The role of emotion regulation and children's early academic success. *Journal of School Psychology, 45*(1), 3–19. https://doi.org/10.1016/j.jsp.2006.09.002

Greene, R. W. (2021). *The explosive child: A new approach for understanding and parenting easily frustrated, chronically inflexible children* (6th ed.). Harper Paperbacks.

Greene, R., & Winkler, J. (2019). Collaborative & proactive solutions (CPS): A review of research findings in families, schools, and

REFERENCES

treatment facilities. *Clinical Child and Family Psychology Review, 22*(4), 549–561. https://doi.org/10.1007/s10567-019-00295-z

Harvey, P., & Penzo, J. (2009). *Parenting a child who has intense emotions*. New Harbinger Publications.

Huebner, D. (2007). *What to do when your temper flares*. Magination Press.

Iannaccone, J. A., & Jessel, J. (2021). A translational comparison of contingency-based progressive delay procedures and their effects on contextually appropriate behavior. *Journal of Applied Behavior Analysis, 54*(1), 231–247. https://doi.org/10.1002/jaba.780

Jin, C. S., Hanley, G. P., & Beaulieu, L. (2013). An individualized and comprehensive approach to treating sleep problems in young children. *Journal of Applied Behavior Analysis, 46*(1), 161–180. https://doi.org/10.1002/jaba.16

Kazdin, A. E. (2014). *The everyday parenting toolkit: The Kazdin method for easy, step-by-step, lasting change for you and your child*. Harper Paperbacks.

Kelly, A. N., Axe, J. B., Allen, R. F., & Maguire, R. W. (2015). Effects of presession pairing on the challenging behavior and academic responding of children with autism. *Behavioral Interventions, 30*(2), 135–156. https://doi.org/10.1002/bin.1408

Kumar Muppalla, S., Vuppalapati, S., Reddy Pulliahgaru, A., & Sreenivasulu, H. (2023). Effects of excessive screen time on child development: An updated review and strategies for management. *Cureus, 15*(6), e40608. https://doi.org/10.7759/cureus.40608

Kuypers, L. (2011). *The zones of regulation*. Think Social Publishing, Inc.

Lu, D., & Gao, X. (2023). The effect of the time parents spend with children on children's well-being. *Frontiers in Psychology, 14*, Article 123456. https://doi.org/10.3389/fpsyg.2023.1096128

Lucas-Molina, B., Quintanilla, L., Sarmento-Henrique, R., Martín Babarro, J., & Giménez-Dasí, M. (2020). The relationship between emotion regulation and emotion knowledge in preschoolers: A longitudinal study. *International Journal of Environmental Research and Public Health, 17*(16), 5726. https://doi.org/10.3390/ijerph17165726

McGuirk, R. (2024, September 10). Australia proposes legal minimum age for accessing social media. *ABC News*. https://www.ctvnews.ca/world/australia-proposes-legal-minimum-age-for-children-accessing-social-media-1.7031925

Murthy, V. (2023). *Social media and youth mental health*. Office of the Surgeon General. https://www.hhs.gov/sites/default/files/sg-youth-mental-health-social-media-advisory.pdf

Murthy, V. (2024, June 17). Surgeon General: Why I'm calling for a warning label on social media platforms. *The New York Times*. https://www.nytimes.com/2024/06/17/opinion/social-media-health-warning.html

National Sleep Foundation. (2020, November 12). *What are the sleep stages?* https://www.thensf.org/what-are-the-sleep-stages/

Ontario Newsroom. (2024, April 28). *Ontario cracking down on cellphone use and banning vaping in schools*. https://news.ontario.

REFERENCES

ca/en/release/1004501/ontario-cracking-down-on-cellphone-use-and-banning-vaping-in-schools

Paley, B., & Hajal, N. J. (2022). Conceptualizing emotion regulation and co-regulation as a family-level phenomenon. *Clinical Child and Family Psychology Review, 25*(1), 19–43. https://doi.org/10.1007/s10567-022-00378-4

Raising Children Network Australia. (2022, December 19). *Using screen time and digital technology for learning: Children and pre-teens*. https://raisingchildren.net.au/school-age/school-learning/learning-ideas/screen-time-helps-children-learn

Shaw P., Stringaris A., Nigg J., & Leibenluft E. (2014). Emotion dysregulation in attention deficit hyperactivity disorder. *American Journal of Psychiatry, 171*(3), 276–293. https://doi.org/10.1176/appi.ajp.2013.13070966

Tarbox, C., Tarbox, J., Bermudez, T. L., Silverman, E., & Servellon, L. (2023). Kind extinction: A procedural variation on traditional extinction. *Behavior Analysis in Practice*. https://doi.org/10.1007/s40617-023-00833-w

Tiger, J. H., Hanley, G. P., & Bruzek, J. (2008). Functional communication training: A review and practical guide. *Behavior Analysis in Practice, 1*(1), 16–23. https://doi.org/10.1007%2FBF03391716

VanDevander, J., Warner, A., Kazemi, E., & Fahmie, T. (2024). Creating a reference range of common problem behaviors and replacement behaviors in neurotypical children. *Behavioral Interventions, 39*(1), Article e1978. https://doi.org/10.1002/bin.1978

Index

A

accepting no for an answer. *See* no
acknowledgement. *See* attention, getting the child's
actions, how to teach   74–82
aggression, aggressive behaviour   173, 227, 235
   physical   130, 264
   scenarios   67–68, 71–72
alternatives, problem behaviour and   106–07
anger, parental   68, 140–41
anger in children   156, 157, 227, 242
   scenarios   67, 184
   see also tantrums
antecedent prompt   69, 72
attention, getting the child's   163–64, 167, 170
attention-seeking   32–33, 42, 49, 56–57
   at bedtime   256, 260
   scenarios   124, 125, 128
   see also Quality Time

B

backward chaining   78–79
baseline data   159–60
bedwetting   266
behaviour, increase in positive   87
behaviour, problem   121–22
   reinforcement as tool for   106–08
   strategies for dealing with   122–28
   and teachable moments   82
behavioural momentum   168
being nice   11, 22–23, 29, 106, 189

INDEX

  functional communication and   69, 71, 72
  scenarios   26, 28
body language, emotion regulation and   232, 233
break, taking a   235, 240–41
bribery, bribing   97–99

C

Canadian Pediatric Society sleep guidelines   268–69
Cat Nap (sleep stage)   247
catch them being good   24–25, 28, 29, 101, 187
checklists   74–77
  morning routines and   201–02, 203–04
choice(s)   19–21, 27, 29, 170, 186
chores, scenarios and strategies   17, 88–89, 97–98, 113
clarity (spelling it out)   18–19, 29, 30, 200–01, 230
  saying no   187
  scenarios   27, 28
Collaborative and Proactive Solutions   48–49
communication, functional   67–70
compliance   159–60
  fake   157
  see also co-operation
consequences   104, 121, 122
  natural   137–38, 170
  screen time and   217–18
contract, screen time   211–13, 217, 222–23
co-operation (compliance)   155–59, 182
  baseline data   159–60
  games and   177
  non-co-operation   156–57, 172–79
  and punishment   179
  scenarios   154–55, 180–81
  and sleep training   264
  teaching   161–74
  time-out and   178–79
coping strategies. *See* emotion regulation
co-regulation   237–39
co-sleeping   244–45
credibility   142

D

deadlines. *See* morning routines
Deep Sleep (sleep stage)   247
defiance (non-co-operation)   156–58
  scenarios   123–25
Differential Reinforcement   107

281

E

effort, response effort   111–12
emotion regulation   224–41
  and body language   232, 233
  co-regulation   237–39
  modelling   236–37
  role play (practise)   239–42
  as teachable skill   227–29, 231–32, 235–41
  tools for   235–36
  validation   232–34
emotion regulation/dysregulation
  resources   243
  statistics   226–27
energy and (intensity)   102
environment, sleep   250, 255
expectations   11–12, 18–19, 30, 140, 185
  emotional regulation and   228–29
  rewards and   104
extinction burst   126–27, 147–48
extinction strategy   122–23, 123–25

F

fading   71, 79, 81, 92, 107–08, 204–05
Ferberizing (Dr Ferber)   257, 258
First .... then   77–78, 172
  see also If - then
flexibility   23, 40, 41, 93
  screen time and   216, 219, 221
follow-through   172
freebies, privileges   23–24, 28, 29
Functional Communication (FCT)   67–70

G

games, co-operation and   177
Generalization   196
grandparent, give like a   22, 29, 30

H

hangry scenario   67–70
Hanley, Dr Greg   257
Harvey, Pat and Jeanine Penzo *(Parenting a Child Who Has Intense Emotions)*   243
heads-up   21–22, 26, 27, 29, 168, 187
  emotion regulation and   230–31
  and screens   177–78
Health Canada, sleep statistics   246
Huebner, Dawn *(What to Do When Your Temper Flares)*   243

INDEX

I

If.... then 77, 170–71
  see also First - then
ignoring 47, 156, 158, 163, 174
  and bribery 97
  as parent 15, 106, 121, 147, 148
    see also extinction
immediacy, reinforcement and 89, 91–92, 101, 106, 137, 182
instructions, delivering effective 165–74
  see also co-operation
intensity (energy and) 102
  see also Differential Reinforcement
Intermittent Reinforcement 108, 195

K

KISS principle 169
Kuypers, Leah *(Zones of Regulation)* 243

L

labelling as validation 233

M

manners 19, 70, 171
mealtimes 11–12, 19, 70
  scenarios 154–55
mental health, social media and 215
modelling 69, 71, 81–82
  emotion regulation 238–39
  healthy screen use 208–09
  positive coping skills 236–37
morning routines 199–203
motivation 85–86, 87, 92, 101–02, 116–17
  internal 114–15
  sleep training and 261–62

N

National Sleep Foundation sleep cycles (stages) 247–48
negative reinforcement 138–39
negotiation (non-co-operation) 104–05, 157
  punishment and 150
nightmares 245, 265
nighttime routines 248–49, 255–56
no (accepting no for an answer) 188–97
  scenarios 183–84, 186, 190, 193–94
  screen time and 218
  statistics 185

strategies for teaching 185–86, 197–98
Non-Contingent Reinforcement 34

O

Operational Definition 18
options. *See* choices

P

pairing 23–24, 163–64
pare it down 10–12, 29
Parenting a Child Who Has Intense Emotions (Harvey, Pat and Jeanine Penzo) 243
Parenting Journal notes 29–30, 39–40, 60–61, 95–96, 160, 196–98, 203–04, 240–41
partners, co-parenting 134, 140, 150–51, 178
pets, children and 17, 64–65, 123, 125
physical proximity 80–81
pick your battles 13–17, 26, 29, 165, 185
Positive Opposites 50–52, 67, 69, 71–72
    emotion regulation and 235–36, 240–41
Positive Reinforcement 71, 72, 84–89, 91–92, 171–72
    80/20 rule 104–05, 142
    dos and don'ts 89–91, 101–08
    reality checks 99–100
    reinforcers, types of 92–95, 204–05, 211–12
        saying yes after no 190–91
    synthesized reinforcement 96–97
    troubleshooting 110–15, 258
    v punishment 116–17
Power Nap (sleep stage) 247
practice, practising 69, 164, 202, 239–41
praise 101–02, 106, 121, 241–42
    multiple instructions and 175
    negative response to 112–13
    see also positive reinforcement
preparation, prepare strategies 6–7, 10–11, 200
privileges, removal of 134–36
proactive mindset 9–10
problem behaviours. *See* behaviour, problem
procrastination 50, 57
Progressive Waiting (sleep training) 257–61
    schedules 258, 267–68, 269–70
prompting 69, 71, 72, 77, 79–81
punishment 116–17, 118–20
    considerations (dos) 129, 139–144, 145–46
    emotional, physical 130–31
    emotions and 242–43
    escalating cycles of 143–44, 148–49
    troubleshooting 146–51, 179

INDEX

Q

Quality Time 24, 31–37
  essentials of 37–41
  punishment and 149
  and sleep training 256
  troubleshooting 41–44

R

reactions 66–67
  see also Co-operation; Functional Communication
reactive approaches 13, 32–33
realistic expectations. *See* expectations
reality checks 59–60, 95–96, 99–100
reasonableness 12, 55, 129, 145–46, 159, 185, 229
  screen time and 210, 219
refusal (non-co-operation). *See* defiance
reinforcement. *See* Positive Reinforcement
REM Sleep (sleep stage) 248
requests (from children) 69, 71–73
  screen time and 216
resources, emotion regulation 243
rewards 70
  finding appropriate 103–04, 110–11, 171
  increased demand for 113, 176–77
  morning routines and 202–03
  see also praise; reinforcement
role play (practise), emotional regulation and 239–40
routines, nighttime. *See* nighttime routines

S

screens, screen time 206–08
  contract 211–12, 217–18
    template 222–23
  monitoring, sharing 212–13, 214–15, 220
  removal of 134
  transitioning from 177–78, 216
  troubleshooting 16, 218–20
  WHO guidelines 210–11
shaping 70
skills, identifying and teaching 49, 53–60
  see also actions, how to teach
sleep 244–45
  dependencies 249–54, 261
  guidelines and statistics 246, 247–48, 250, 268–69
sleep training 254–62
  nighttime routines 248–49

troubleshooting 253, 263–68
SMART goals 64–66
social media and mental health 215
spelling it out. *See* clarity
statistics, sleep (children) 246
sticker charts 84, 87
synthesized reinforcement 96–97

T

talking trap (too much information) 169, 176
tantrums 68
   and accepting no 189
   accidental rewarding of 114
   scenarios 50, 54–55, 57–58, 89, 123, 125, 127
   screens and 177–78
   see also anger
tasks. *See* actions, how to teach
teachable moments 63, 82
teaching 46–49
   strategies and techniques 62–66
   see also actions; co-operation; functional communication
tell, don't ask 165, 168–69
tidying up, scenarios and strategies 13–14, 52, 53–54, 81–82
time-out 131–34, 178–79
timers, use of 132, 168, 212–13, 266
   and sleep training 260–61
timing 97, 166–67
   sleep training and 256
transition away from screens. *See* screens
treasure chests (rewards) 103, 110
tuning out 156, 163
   see also ignoring

V

validation (of feelings) 232–35
visual schedules. *See* checklists
voice, volume of 174

W

waiting 192–95
   see also Progressive Waiting (sleep training)
What to Do When Your Temper Flares (Huebner, Dawn) 243
World Health Organisation (WHO) screen time guidelines 210–11

Z

Zones of Regulation (Kuypers, Leah) 243

www.ingramcontent.com/pod-product-compliance
Lightning Source LLC
Chambersburg PA
CBHW061934220426
43662CB00012B/1907